NCMC
BR
121.2
.A73
1987

1722004Z

A Call to Discernment

Jay E. Adams

D0104484

HARVEST HOUSE PUBLISHERS
Eugene, Oregon 97402

Except where otherwise indicated, all Scripture quotations in this book are taken from the New American Standard Bible, © The Lockman Foundation 1960, 1962, 1963, 1968, 1971, 1972, 1973, 1975, 1977. Used by permission.

A CALL TO DISCERNMENT

Copyright © 1987 by Harvest House Publishers
Eugene, Oregon 97402

Library of Congress Catalog Card Number 87-081038
ISBN 0-89081-588-7

All rights reserved. No portion of this book may be reproduced in any form without the written permission of the Publisher.

Printed in the United States of America.

To Bill

Keep on growing in discernment!

INTRODUCTION

Today the church is confused. Siren voices call to her from every side. False teaching and heresy abound. Many Christians fall prey, because they simply do not know how to distinguish truth from error. Slogans are bandied about: "All truth is God's truth." Naturally, if it is truth it is God's. No one in his right mind would deny that. But it is also a fact that "all error is the devil's error." Now where are we? Back to square one. We must still distinguish God's truth from the devil's error; sloganizing won't do that for us. What is wrong? Why is the church so susceptible to falsehood? What can be done about it? Where does one turn for help?

That is what this book is all about: how *you* can become part of the solution rather than part of the problem. I say "you" because the church *is* you, you and thousands of others like you. The church will not change en masse, but only as individual Christians like you change. And what the church—you and your brothers and sisters in Christ—needs to solve the problem is *spiritual discernment*.

In this book I intend to show how serious a problem lack of discernment is today, and to demonstrate some of the effects of this lack. I want to explain exactly what spiritual discernment is and why it is lacking. Finally, I propose to show how you can become a more discerning Christian.

In order to do this I have set forth a program by which you may become a more discerning Christian. Use it *flexibly*. Perhaps you will find it helpful to follow the program together with other Christians. Possibly you may wish to use it in a Sunday school class or Bible study group. It is adaptable. Sometimes it is wise—at least at the beginning—to work together with other people. Hearing several viewpoints other than your own can be helpful, provided they are based on adequate biblical study and are not merely the pooling of ignorance and sheer opinion.

But for the greatest benefit, do the work yourself instead of leaning on others to provide answers for you. Much profitable, individual time in the Scriptures is necessary to become the discerning Christian that God wants you to be. Sooner or later you must learn to work on your own. You will not always have others to turn to when you must make decisions and discover God's answers. So, while all sorts of adaptations are possible, the program as it stands is designed to enable you to become a strong Christian, capable of discerning the will of the Lord.

—Jay E. Adams
Valley Center, CA
1986

CONTENTS

1

The Lack of
Spiritual Discernment

1

The Lack of
Spiritual Discernment

Back in the early 1950's, when I was beginning my ministry, an enthusiastic mother showed me some children's books which she had just bought from a door-to-door salesman. "Aren't they beautiful, pastor?" she gushed. "I'm so excited I can hardly wait to begin reading them to my children!"

What this mother didn't realize was that these books she had just purchased from a door-to-door salesman were published by the Seventh-Day Adventist Church and contained many of the distinctive doctrines of that church. "How can I gently deflate her balloon?" I wondered. In response I casually said, "My, don't the Seventh-Day Adventists put out attractive materials! Just look at those lovely pictures!"

"What?" she exclaimed. "This is Seventh-Day Adventist material? He didn't tell me that!"

In the 30-odd years since that incident I have come to realize that the problem I was then confronting— lack of discernment—is one of the principal problems that pastors face. Perhaps more church fights, splits, and conflicts originate in someone's lack of discernment than from any other source. In every area of life, members of the church are continually bombarded with ideas, beliefs, and opinions, most of which are unbiblical or at least biblically suspect. But they don't know how to sort things out. Often the church itself contributes to the problem by sending conflicting and erroneous messages. Truly, confusion reigns.

Right and Wrong Responses

Recently, Christians were chagrined to learn of the scandal involving Jim and Tammy Bakker, hosts of the PTL Club and directors of a vast satellite network and the empire connected with it in South Carolina.

Many people have come alive to the fact that they uncritically gave money to this club, 265,000 dollars of which they are now told was used as a payoff to Jessica Hahn, with whom Bakker admittedly had an affair. That exposé coincided with Oral Roberts' unprecedented plea for 4.5 million dollars by March 31, 1987, based on the premise that if he didn't receive it by that date God would take his life. Everywhere I travel, I hear Christians talking about these events.

Was this confluence of events "pure chance," as *Time* magazine suggests?[1] Or has God, in His wise providence and infinite goodness, sent a message to His church? Is He telling you and those all around you to awaken to what has been going on? Is He calling us all to account for what we have allowed to happen by our uncritical support? In short, is He calling His church to discernment?

The tragic response of many people, when faced with scandals like these, is to become cynical and embittered. That is wrong. God doesn't want us to throw away the good with the bad, the genuine with the false; He wants us to learn to distinguish between the two. There has been too much uncritical lethargy,

too much following the crowd, and too much willing-
ness to be deceived. It is "easier" that way.

But God rarely bids us take the easy way. He wants us
to work at our faith. He wants us not merely to pray
but to "*watch* and pray" (in Matthew 26:41 the word
"watch" means to *be alert*). And we must be alert not
only to the large, media-intensive events; the problem
is all around—in the home and in the local church.

Take, for example, the church lending library. Frequently it is the repository for the most extraordinary
accumulation of discarded artifacts donated over the
years by members after cleaning out their attics. One
pastor tells this story:

> I served an evangelical church as one of the
> seven pastors for several years. The church is
> located in the Midwest and has a membership
> in excess of 4000. The church has a lending
> library with about 2500 volumes.
>
> It became increasingly obvious that a wide
> divergence of books by liberals, conserva-
> tives, charismatics, and even unbelievers was
> in that library. Discernment was left to the
> church member with no selective help from
> the church.
>
> Looking through the card catalog index
> showed us what books the people were bor-
> rowing. What a surprise that was! We sur-
> mised that the apparent theological imma-
> turity of the congregation was in some way
> directly related to the resources they had
> available and were encouraged to use.
>
> After much concern and debate, the few
> members of the 17-member staff who were

genuinely concerned were able to get the library to agree to add those volumes we thought were needed and to place disclaimers in books that we could convince the senior pastor were not really in keeping with what our church should provide as reading material for our people. We were placated.

So much for the church-library problem! Consider another problem described by a Bible-believing pastor:

I want to tell you about a radio station located in the suburb of a large metropolitan city. It is owned and operated by an individual who is a member of an evangelical congregation. One of his programs is a daily drive-time talk show. The purpose of the show is to provide the listener with helpful hints on a variety of needs and ideas for the home, garden, or hobby. The host, who has been on the radio scene for nearly 25 years, has a strong following on the talk-show circuit. I was listening to the show one morning in July of 1986 when a caller ended her conversation on the air by saying, "The Lord bless you." The host was silent for several seconds. Then he replied, "I wish people wouldn't say that kind of stuff on the radio. I don't think it is right to assume that someone else may hold your religious beliefs. What if I were a Jew? Or an Arab? After all, there's not just one way to God. I don't know how you feel, but that's what I think."

When contacted, the owner of the station said that the views of the host are not necessarily those of the station! He said that by keeping him on the air some of the people will choose to remain tuned to the station and hear the gospel.

Was he right? Will they choose to believe that host? What about those who lack discernment? What will they think?

Combating Confusion

While living in Georgia, I listened to a "converted" Roman Catholic priest for days in a row denounce the doctrine of the Trinity as "pagan"—in his program on a "Christian" radio station! On another occasion, while driving through Texas, I heard a preacher invite listeners to "stay tuned to this program because at the end of the message I will tell you how to obtain an autographed picture of Jesus Christ." I couldn't believe my ears. I was certain that I had misunderstood. So I stayed tuned, and sure enough at the end he repeated his offer, telling us where to send for the autographed picture and encouraging us to include a gift for his "ministry."

People—genuine Christians—whom you wouldn't suspect of falling for such nonsense nevertheless have become confused. Jesus warned us about "false prophets who come to you in sheep's clothing but within are greedy wolves" (Matthew 7:15). Christians with little discernment have failed to heed His warning. Why is that? And what can you do about it?

Frequently I hold conferences for people who want to advance biblical counseling. But so often when I look at the book table they set up for the conference, I find materials for sale that teach all kinds of things contrary to the design of the conference. I can only wonder at the lack of discernment (or concern about it) evidenced by the sponsors of the conference. Do they really know the difference between truth and error in biblical counseling? Do they even care?

A few weeks ago I was invited to contrast biblical truth with the errors of the teaching of the Maslow/Third Force self-esteem movement. From the tract rack of the church holding the meeting I picked up a tract entitled "How Valuable Am I?" that teaches the very doctrines I had been asked to refute. For example, this tract says that Jesus "seems to have an exceptionally high value upon you. After all, He thought you were so valuable that He laid down His life in your behalf. He was crucified, buried, and raised again because of the tremendous value He lays upon you." Such teaching is heresy. It denies what the Bible says about God's grace. It was not because we were of such tremendous value to God that He sent His son to die for us; rather, in spite of the fact that we were His "enemies" (Romans 5:10) Christ died for us. To say that what moved God to send Christ was our great value is to deny everything that the Bible teaches about our utter unworthiness and the unmerited love of God.

In this particular case, as so often is true, the tract was published and distributed by the denomination with which the congregation is affiliated. So, along with other denominational pamphlets, and without careful evaluation, it was placed in the tract rack. After all, it came from "headquarters." Such blind faith in denominations—even basically good ones—in time often leads to liberalism. Many people leave the thinking to others. They do not learn to discern. "After all, why bother? My church will take care of those matters." Where are the Bereans today, those believers who diligently examined the Scriptures to see if what Paul and Silas taught was true (Acts 17:11).

Recently I received a Christmas catalog in the mail from a local Christian bookstore in which books by Francis Schaeffer and Robert Schuller are equally commended to us as gifts to present to our friends and loved ones. What sort of discernment is displayed in the selection of these items?

A couple of years ago I attended a Bible-believing church and discovered that the pastor was not preaching that night. Instead, we were "treated" to a film on self-esteem—put out by the Mormons.

Then there is music! Music is effective in creating moods and in conveying messages. But how many Christians ever think about what they are listening to or singing? If it isn't rock or some other obviously objectionable number, Christians just join in. In perhaps the most carefully prepared hymnal in the United States, you can still find Edmund Sears' Christmas carol "It Came Upon the Midnight Clear," with all of its objectionable theology. One verse straightforwardly teaches pagan cosmology based on a cyclical view of history: "With the ever-circling years comes round the age of gold." Do you talk with the dead? Then why do you sing another song about holding "mystic sweet communion with those whose rest is won"?

Still staying away from the grosser "Christian rock," consider a couple of lines from gospel music in books used by youth groups. In one song the words require the singer to sing ecstatically about "falling on my knees with my face to the rising sun." What on earth does that mean? Have Christians become sun-worshipers? In another song worshipers are to encourage one another with these words: "Now expect a miracle and a miracle is yours today." According to the theology taught in that line, God is always at the disposal of His people, obligated to work miracles for them whenever they expect Him to. How must the son of a cancer victim feel when his mother dies even though he expected a miraculous cure but didn't get it after he has sung those words in your youth group week after week?

Good Causes, Wrong Approaches

A few years back, an acquaintance attempted to bring me together with a man who claimed to have a ministry of postabortion counseling. His method, as he explained it to me, was to direct the mother to ask God whether the aborted child was a girl or boy. Then, my friend said, he directed her to name the child and ask its forgiveness. In the name of Christ, this man was engaged in spiritism. My acquaintance apparently lacked the discernment to know that we could never join forces and work together!

While speaking of abortion, it is sad to notice how in their desire to thwart the abortion movement many well-meaning Christians unintentionally exalt man by declaring him to be of infinite worth. Abortion should not be fought on the basis that killing a human being is wrong because he or she is so valuable, but on the basis that, when a child bearing God's image is slaughtered, it is *God* who is attacked because that child bears His image. If you tear up a picture of my wife, you'll have me to answer to—not because of the intrinsic worth or value of the paper and print that you destroyed, but because you have insulted my wife. An attack on the image of God is serious, not because of man's supposed great worth, but because of the One whose image he reflects. Yet undiscerning Christians, some of whom have good discernment when it comes to other things, seem to fall apart in their thinking at this point. A discerning Christian is careful that statements he makes at one point do not contradict what he says at another. He thinks systematically about his faith.

There are those Christians who laud Alcoholics Anonymous because "their method works" or because "they are doing so much good." Little do they realize that AA insults the true God in its 12 steps by allowing participants to acknowledge any "power greater than myself" as god. Nor is there any discernment of the fact that AA's help is far different from the help offered to drunkards in the Bible. It takes spiritual discernment to understand the great difference between AA telling members that they will always be alcoholics who must fight against drunkenness every day the rest of their lives and the apostle Paul writing of those who in Christ have put off drunkenness once and for all (1 Corinthians 6:9ff.). Moreover, it takes spiritual discernment to realize that a person may enter AA as a drunkard who is heading for hell and may leave sober but still headed for hell. True discernment acknowledges as biblical only the help that meets the needs of the whole person—physical, emotional, and spiritual. Further, even sharper discernment is required to recognize the fact that a "reformed" drunkard who has not come to know Christ as his Savior is probably farther from the kingdom than he was before. The propaganda incessantly spouted forth from radio and television tells us that drunkenness is only a disease. It shouldn't take even *spiritual* discernment to understand that this is little more than euphemistic language designed to take in the culpable. If drunkenness is a disease, so is cocaine abuse. The Bible clearly calls it sin, but in spite of that fact any number of Christians are confused.

The Big Issue

It would not surprise me if some of you reading this chapter are becoming restive and uncomfortable, and even a few are growing angry. This is to be expected because, apart from discernment, these matters seem inconsequential. Indeed, they may seem petty and unworthy of discussion. "Why not concern one's self with the big issues?" you may ask.

I *am* concerned with the big issue: the careless, undiscriminating mentality that lies behind the kinds of problems I have raised. Actually, they are only symptoms of the larger problem, which in turn grows out of a mentality that says, "It's fanatical to constantly be at this matter of distinguishing and differentiating; you can't go through life that way." When we examine the reasons for this widespread lack of discernment, we shall see that the biblical concept of antithesis is rarely taught anymore in our churches. Yet this concept is plainly evident in the Bible. For example, the "clean/unclean" requirements of the Old Testament distinguished such things as foods the Israelites could or could not eat and what kinds of clothing they could or could not wear. God's people were expected to be concerned every day about all they did—even in the little things. They were to go through life distinguishing God's way from what is not God's way. Yet today such biblical thinking has been replaced by a mentality that permits no sharp contrasts. All is gray: There is no black or white, good or bad, right or wrong. Those who try to think and live according to biblical ideals are accused of majoring on picayune concerns.

I once visited a Sunday school class in a Bible-believing church in Missouri where the teacher said, "I prefer to think of God the Father as having a body. It makes Him more real to me." Not a single member of the large class that attentively soaked up his words objected to this heretical concept. Is it petty to notice such things? Not when God has plainly told us that He is a Spirit and has warned us against reducing Him to some idolatrous form represented by one of His creatures.

Listening to Christians talk, watching them purchase materials in Christian bookstores, and hearing their comments about sermons and radio broadcasts is like observing a color-blind painter trying to distinguish chips on a color chart. The effect of their lack of discernment is often like that of a tone-deaf singer in a congregation whose singing throws everyone around him off key.

The sheer quantity and variety of religious output today, to say nothing of non-Christian offerings from untold sources, fairly screams for Christians to develop sharper powers of discernment. So much chaff must be removed in order to get at the wheat! Proverbs 10:19 warns that where there are many words, sin is inevitable. Yet little is said about the lack of discernment in church; indeed, to my knowledge this is the first book on the subject. What is worse, there seems to be even less concern than in days gone by, when the problem was less acute. Sometimes Christians look back on those days and congratulate themselves about how much broader and tolerant the evangelical church has become today. While there were certainly some things that needed improvement, we have gone far beyond improvement in our laissez-faire approach to Christianity and the truth of God's Word. This book is not a call to return to past errors but it is a summons to Christians everywhere to become more discriminating about their beliefs.

Write What Is True

This is also a challenge for more accurate writing. Book reviews and analyses in magazines and journals often so seriously misrepresent facts and distort a person's views that one can only wonder whether reviewers and commentators have actually read what was written. For example, a seminary professor was quoted in *Moody Monthly* as saying, "And the popular writings of Gary Collins, James Dobson, and Jay Adams have helped build a bridge between evangelical thinking and psychology." No wonder the person who sent me the clipping in which this quotation appears circled it and wrote "Good grief!" Gary Collins? Yes. James Dobson? Certainly. But me? What can the speaker (if quoted accurately) be thinking?

Such ludicrous things happen all the time. Sometimes they are only a slip of the tongue, but too often they are not. The Christian public reads and gobbles up all too much of this material without even thinking to think. Then, from a conglomerate store of such misinformation, disinformation, distortion, and truth, Christians try to sort out life, all the while making bad decisions and getting themselves into a peck of trouble.

Others grow more and more immobile, not knowing what to believe or think. No wonder there is so much confusion in the church today: There is so little discernment!

Thousands of Christians cannot discern between what is biblical counseling and what is not. They do not know how to distinguish between Christian counseling (counseling that is truly Christian in content and method) and a Christian doing counseling (that may or may not be Christian in content and method). Consequently they are being drawn into psychological error by the bus-full. Apropos to this fact, in his *Christian Information Bureau Bulletin* of July 1986 (p. 1) Dave Hunt wrote:

> Christian psychology represents the most deadly and at the same time the most appealing and popular form of *modernism* ever to confront the church. Those who refuse the temptation to adjust Biblical interpretation to agree with Darwin have succumbed to the even more deadly delusion of integrating Freud and Jung into Christianity. It is astonishing that so many of today's evangelical leaders, in order to be "relevant," are preaching a form of Science of Mind without even recognizing it.

The last four words of the quotation say it well: Preachers and other leaders are being lured away from the truths of Scripture *without even recognizing it.* How can that be? It is the result of a failure to cultivate in leaders, and in those who follow them, that spiritual discernment which every Christian needs in order to think and act in ways that please God. If leaders don't even recognize what is happening to them, what can we expect from their people?

Why is there so little discernment—such inability to distinguish things that differ? How did this sad state of affairs come about? What contributes to it? Can anything be done to rectify the situation? Come with me through the chapters that follow as I give you my answers to those questions.

2

What Caused
This Lack?

2

What Caused This Lack?

Many varying but related elements have converged to bring about the church's current widespread lack of spiritual discernment. I shall discuss several of the proximate causes, and then I want to look at one fundamental factor from which they all flow.

Disappearing Church Discipline

Perhaps the most obvious difficulty, once you become aware of it, is the collapse of church discipline. When the church is actively at work caring for its members, as it should by applying the healing balm of church discipline, discernment grows. It grows both among those who are disciplined and those who administer the discipline.

Discipline, by its very nature, requires discernment. Discipline calls for discrimination—distinguishing between those who are right and those who are wrong (and in what ways) in particular cases. Ultimately, in church discipline, you determine who must be retained and who must be put out of the church. Such activities, when properly pursued, cannot be carried out in a sloppy, unthinking way. Equally, in all that it does, the disciplining body must show concern for the honor of God's name, the welfare of the congregation, and the reclamation of the offender. It must be neither soft nor harsh. Such balance calls for spiritual discernment of the highest sort. So-called "petty" issues are seen in their true light as rebellion against Christ's authority vested in His church when they come under the focus of church discipline. Gossip, slander, and false accusations must be rejected and dealt with. Evidence must be weighed. Decisions of momentous import must be made. So, as you can see, the very process of church discipline is largely a process of discernment.[1]

But mostly what I want to observe is that lack of discernment and lack of church discipline walk side by side. Not only does the same mentality lead to both lacks, but by rejecting discipline one naturally downplays the very concerns that make him discerning. When churches overreacted to the abuse of discipline that was all too common in the eighteenth and nineteenth centuries by virtually eliminating church discipline, the broken dike cleared the way for the liberal takeover of the church and allowed the ways of the world to flood in.

Church discipline erects a barrier between the church and the world; when it is removed, it becomes impossible to distinguish the two. With the removal of this barrier, the church was inundated by persons whose profession of faith was at best suspect. These marginal persons brought new concerns, perspectives, and attitudes into the church and directed her into different pathways. The church, to a great extent, began to think and act like the world. As the church became secularized, interest in spiritual discernment waned.

Why should distinctions and differences be of significance? The great thing was to make Christianity as much like the world as possible. The church began to seek the world's approval and adopted her ways rather than standing against them. In this way the perceived need for discernment was lessened.

Continuum Versus Antithesis

With church discipline in ruins, the line between the church and the world smudged, and the church's shift of concern toward friendship with the world well established, the biblical concept of antithesis all but vanished. People who study the Bible in depth develop antithetical mindsets: They think in terms of contrasts or opposites. From Genesis to Revelation God's thoughts and ways are set over against all others. The Bible does not teach that there are numerous ways to please God, each of which is as good as the next. Nor does it teach that various opinions are more or less God's ways. What it teaches—everywhere—is that any thought or way that is not wholly God's is altogether wrong and must be rejected. According to the Bible, a miss is as good as a mile. There is only one God, and there is only one way of life—His!

People today don't like to hear such things—even people within the church. Why? Because they have a different mindset. Many of them have not known the Bible from childhood or ever made an intensive study of it later on, so their mindset is unbiblical. Modern mentality, even in the church (too often *taught* by the church and Christian schools), is a continuum mentality: Truth and values are not absolute but relative.

Such thinking predominates in our culture. Stop and reflect for a moment: What kind of mindset do you have? Do you think in terms of absolutes? Or is life a series of value judgments that vary according to the situation?

According to continuum thinking, the mode of thinking taught outside the church (and largely within), every idea is a shade of gray. There is no right and wrong or true and false, but only shades of right and wrong or true and false spread along a continuum. The poles of this continuum are extended so far out toward the wings that for all practical purposes they are unattainable and therefore worthless. Nothing, then, is wholly right or wrong. All is relative; most of it is subjective.

That is one reason why biblical preaching, with its sharp antithesis, rubs many people the wrong way: It is hard for modern minds to accept. For a long time now educational institutions,[2] newspapers, magazines, radio, TV, etc. have inculcated continuum thinking. Antithetical thinking is dismissed as fanatical or worse. Consequently, when Christians (all of whom have been affected by this environment) hear antithetical views expressed, they sound discordant. And indeed they are! Because anything goes, discernment is not placed at a premium. The word selected to describe racism was *discrimination*. Prior to that it was a compliment to call a person discriminating. If the true cannot be distinguished from the false, the right from the wrong, the good from the bad, then discernment is not only unattainable but it is unnecessary, and its pursuit is foolishness. Discernment thrives in an atmosphere of absolutes, among people whose minds have been molded to think antithetically.

In the Bible, where antithesis is so important, discernment—the ability to distinguish God's thoughts and God's ways from all others—is essential. Indeed, God says that "the wise in heart will be called discerning" (Proverbs 16:21).

From the Garden of Eden with its two trees (one allowed, one forbidden) to the eternal destiny of the human being in heaven or in hell, the Bible sets forth two, and only two, ways: God's way, and all others. Accordingly, people are said to be saved or lost. They belong to God's people or the world. There was Gerizim, the mount of blessing, and Ebal, the mount of cursing. There is the narrow way and the wide way, leading either to eternal life or to destruction. There are those who are against and those who are with us, those within and those without. There is life and death, truth and falsehood, good and bad, light and darkness, the kingdom of God and the kingdom of Satan, love and hatred, spiritual wisdom and the wisdom of the world. Christ is said to be the way, the truth, and the life, and no one may come to the Father but by Him. His is the only name under the sky by which one may be saved.

Not only will you find such antithetical teaching, and much more, on nearly every page of the Bible, but even the construction of the Hebrew language itself seems designed to teach antithesis. Much scriptural poetry, many proverbs, and even some narrative is antithetical in structure.

Perhaps you have wondered about the principle underlying the clean/unclean distinctions of the Old Testament. Various rationales have been given for some of these distinctions, yet many seem to be purely arbitrary. May I suggest that all problems of arbitrariness are resolved when you see the clean/unclean system as a means of alerting the Jew to the fact that all day long, every day, in whatever he does, he must consciously choose God's way. Choices about food, clothing, farming techniques, justice, health care, holidays, and methods of worship were made either God's way or some other way. In other words, the clean/unclean system was designed to develop in God's people an antithetical mentality. Forbidding the mixing of materials in clothing, for example, doesn't seem so arbitrary after all when considered in the light of the biblical concern to create an antithetical posture toward life.

But with pastors and people alike growing up in an environment that stresses continuum thinking, antithesis is dulled as more and more people attempt to integrate sociology, psychology, and business management principles with Scripture. Teachers in Christian colleges now consider it "one of the key tasks of Christian higher education" to "seek to integrate his [the professor's] faith with his learning."[3] The key task, you see, no longer is *to distinguish God's ways* from others but to find places of *agreement* "to the extent to which it is possible."[4] There is a great difference between the two mentalities. According to the one, the task is to find out how one's faith integrates with what he has learned from the world. According to the other, the key task is to determine in what ways a Christian may keep himself unspotted from the world (James 1:27) in both thought and life. He is to remember in all he does that friendship with the world is enmity with God (James 4:4).

In those disciplines for which God did not give us special revelation (while always being careful to discern good from evil at all levels, including the pre-suppositional) the Christian may learn from the world. But his task is not to integrate. Rather, his task is to discover God's truth in what he is doing. His task is to discover how to properly draw the antithesis in reference to his work. He must refine and remold all "learning" according to his fundamental Christian presuppositions and biblical beliefs. He may not merely integrate "learning" as it stands. This is true even of methods, because methods are means committed to the ends of a system. Methods, therefore, must always be considered in the context of the systems they serve. But, in all of this, the important thing to see is that the Christian's task—in whatever he does—is to be sure he is going God's way, a way that is always in antithesis to the world's way ("My thoughts are not your thoughts, neither are your ways My ways"—Isaiah 55:8); he must recognize God's stake in all of life.

That is why the psalmist in Psalm 1:1,2 was concerned, at the very beginning of the psalter, to set forth the two ways: God's and all others, distinguishing them as sharply as he knew how. (He did not try to integrate them!)

The book of Proverbs, at the outset and throughout, does the same thing. The modern educational emphasis on integration is at odds with the educational thrust found in these two biblical textbooks. The biblical axiom is that "the fear of the Lord [belief in and submission to Him] is the beginning of knowledge" (Proverbs 1:7). But this way of thinking is contrary to modern thought, even in the church. In the Bible, Christ and the apostles warn against wolves who attack the flock and urge alertness on the part of elders and pastors who are to protect God's flock (Matthew 7:15). Paul warned the Ephesian elders, "I know that after my departure savage wolves will enter in among you, not sparing the flock, and from among yourselves men will arise speaking distorted things to drag away disciples to follow them" (Acts 20:29,30). The note of antithesis and the need for discrimination is struck in that warning. Christ and the apostles were not constantly involved in controversy and beaten and stoned and killed because they sought agreement with the world and attempted integration wherever possible. They suffered because of the firm, antithetical stand they took for truth over against the world's deceptions. In contrast, today the shift against antithetical thinking and toward humanistic thinking has contributed much to the softness of the church and her frightful lack of discernment.

Deemphasis of Systematic Theology

There was a time when systematic thinking about one's faith was strongly encouraged. Students in seminaries and Bible colleges were taught to think systematically about their faith. Even the laity were taught systematically in churches. This kind of teaching required discernment on everyone's part.

Systematic theology not only looks at what the whole Bible says about any given subject, but it also insists on carefully distinguishing things that differ. Much criticism (not all) about theologians "splitting hairs" is uncalled for and stems from laziness of thought on the part of those who make such disparaging remarks.

This tendency, so prevalent, discourages careful thinking, which in turn allows the "integration" of ideas that are not really systematically self-consistent with one's faith. Moreover, a cavalier attitude toward Scripture has grown up in many corners, a spirit that has led to the use of Scripture to support ideas, beliefs, and practices that are entirely contrary to the Bible as a whole. Nowhere is this tendency more apparent than in Christian counseling.[5]

It is not only a deemphasis on systematic thinking about the faith that has led to the appalling lack of discernment in the church. There is also an overemphasis on the discipline called biblical theology. In some theological institutions this threatens to supplant systematic theology by reducing concern for the finer distinctions of theology in favor of larger, sweeping, less discriminating themes.

Reformation doctrine, the teaching of Protestant reformers such as Luther, Calvin, Zwingli, and others, is ignored as if it never existed or else is renounced as scholastic and sterile. In some places, great doctrines so carefully hammered out over the centuries by exegetical theologians in refutation of heresies are up for grabs. Tradition (good or bad) is discarded as passé and trampled underfoot. Many teachers think they have to invent the theological wheel anew. There is no discernment; the good is tossed aside with the bad.

Self-styled "experts" in psychology, sociology, and education who hold Ph.D.'s in their fields and Sunday school degrees in Bible pontificate on Christian teaching and life on radio and elsewhere, setting themselves up as spokesmen for God. Yet they have never received ordination from the church of Christ to do so.[6] Their teaching and use of the Bible (when it is used) often bear little resemblance to what the Scriptures, properly interpreted, really say.

What is the upshot of all this? One obvious result is the modern tendency to use theological language loosely. Take, for example, the use of the word "miracle." Today everything unusual or extraordinary seems to be called a miracle. When God heals someone through the use of medicine in a marvelous way, we are told that this is a miracle. A careful, theologically defined use of the term would distinguish the marvelous from the miraculous. Should a person whose arm had been amputated sprout a new one in its place, that would be a true miracle. If Joni Eareckson Tada suddenly starts walking after 20 years as a quadriplegic, that would be a miracle. But anything short of this kind of thing should not be considered miraculous.

Not only are biblical terms used imprecisely, thereby spreading confusion throughout the church, but erroneous teachings of every kind are readily tolerated. This is because so few people have the discernment necessary to identify and refute such errors. And if they do sense that something is wrong, their powers of discernment are too weak to put their fingers precisely on the point where the error lies. Or, if they do point out the error, other people denounce them as heresy hunters.

Don't forget how Jesus warmly commended the church at Ephesus for testing those "who call themselves apostles, and aren't" and for finding them "liars" (Revelation 2:2b). There is a place for heresy hunting when done in a biblical manner.

Certainly, neither you nor I want to develop a judgmental spirit. But we must cultivate a discerning spirit. When people quote Matthew 7:1 ("Don't judge or you will be judged") against proper attempts to distinguish and discern truth from error they misuse that important passage, which doesn't forbid all judging but only *improper* judging of the kind you would not care to have applied to you (Matthew 7:2). Indeed, Jesus elsewhere commanded us to "make a right judgment" (John 7:24). Reading further in Matthew 7, you should not fail to notice that the Lord commanded, "Don't give what is holy to dogs, and don't throw your pearls before pigs" (verse 6). To determine who is a pig or dog and who is not requires you to make a judgment. In short, in order to obey that command you must discriminate between pigs who shouldn't hear and people who should. That requires discernment.

In an article in *Training* magazine entitled "On Giving Offense" (Sep. 1986), the editor, Jack Gordon, wrote:

> . . . at some point in the past several years we crossed an invisible line between self-assertion and self-righteousness, and turned into a society of perpetually indignant prigs. . . . I submit that people are entirely too horrified by the possibility of offending someone. . . . I'm talking about the remarkable degree to which we've bought into the premise that the offendee is always right . . . (p. 10).

Yet, as Gordon observes, "our favorite people—the ones we respect—are still those who give it to us straight." He is right! We respect the apostle Paul for that very reason. Gordon certainly has put his finger on a problem in the church: Somehow we have concluded that the supposed offendee is always right.

Well, he isn't! Nor is the supposed offender. We must abandon this outlook and learn to determine who, if anyone, is right or wrong in each case. But that takes discernment.

It is easier, of course, simply to accuse the one who is supposed to have given offense than to determine whether the offendee was sinfully sensitive or proud, and shouldn't have taken offense. But that takes discernment, and discernment is work—hard, exacting work. It runs risks, not the least of which is to suffer vilification. Curiously, it is not thought wrong to upbraid an offender even if he proves that an offendee's anger was sinful. The offendee is immune to censure, it seems, whether he snarls, snaps, or even bites another's heel.

Liberation of the Laity

Much of what we have been discussing goes back to the liberation of the laity. With the rediscovery of the meaning of Ephesians 4:11,12—that God has given officers to His church to equip its members for their work of ministry (an important truth too long covered over by erroneous views of the authority and function of office)—came an overreaction against true authority. (Consider, for example, Hebrews 13:17: "Obey your leaders and submit to them.") The liberation of the laity, with all of the resources and energy that were set loose, has degenerated into anarchy. The laity are to minister, but within the sphere of biblical authority that is invested in the office-bearers of the church—not apart from them. Instead, men and women have arrogated authority to themselves, and have gone off to do whatever is right in their own eyes. As a consequence, individuals with money, or those who are able to gather a following because of their popularity, demand that the church accept their idiosyncratic views —or else. They have weakened the church by draining off funds and personnel into parachurch organizations and "ministries" that compete with her. And they have directly challenged her rights and prerogatives to conduct valid ministry ordained by God by hanging out shingles under which they, in a specialized manner, claim to be able to render "more professional services."

The Christian world has adopted the nefarious practice of merchandising people rather than proclaiming Christ. It has appealed to the groupie spirit that is abroad in the land. There is little or no ability to distinguish between this and the true, God-ordained leadership that is so essential to the welfare of the church.

This is one reason why the scandal associated with some televangelists and spread across the newspapers and magazines of this country was possible. It was fueled by uncritical support from millions of Christians who succumbed to the groupie mentality rather than exercising proper evaluation of both the content and methods of those involved.

Truly, oppressive church government was a pompous evil to which we certainly do not want to return. Nor do we want to see pastors burdened with the task of "doing it all themselves." We are glad for the energy, gifts, and dedication of the laity. Yet in some ways the present situation is every bit as problematic as the former. When unordained persons, subject to no one, and ordained men (who strike out on their own in "ministries" unapproved by their churches) command millions of dollars each year and wield the influence that such money is capable of generating (so that organized churches must either follow their lead or seem inconsequential to their own people), the liberation of the laity has gone too far. In fact, we could almost say that there is a new prelacy abroad today—rule of high-profile personalities who are assuming the role of leadership for the church while operating outside the church and her authority. Along with this new turn of events, discernment has deteriorated. It is put out the door just as surely when "heroic" leaders call the shots as it was when powerful prelates reigned. Thus the liberation of the laity has become a new bondage in which *some* (relatively few) laypersons dominate the people of God and do all the thinking for the rest. When chaos prevails and things are not done decently and in God's order, we are bound by a freedom that has turned into license. This in turn erodes discernment.

Other proximate factors are also leading to the decline of discernment, such as the widespread "feeling" orientation in the church and the deceptive ways in which the enemy packages his products. Yet these four—the disappearance of church discipline, continuum thinking replacing antithesis, the deemphasis of systematic theology, and liberation of the laity—are sufficient to demonstrate that many closely-connected factors play a part.

The Basic Problem

These and other proximate problems that contribute to the present lack of discernment in the church all go back to a much more basic problem. It has been a perennial problem among sinful human beings ever since it was planted by the evil one in the garden. This basic problem is so important that I want to devote a separate chapter to it. But first we must take time to understand thoroughly just what the Bible means by discernment.

3

What Is Spiritual Discernment?

3

What Is
Spiritual Discernment?

In the introduction to his book *The Jeweler's Eye*
William F. Buckley wrote:

> The title is, of course, a calculated effron-
> tery, the relic of an impromptu answer I gave
> once to a tenacious young interviewer who,
> toward the end of a very long session, asked
> me what opinion did I have of myself. I re-
> plied that I thought of myself as a perfectly
> average middle-aged American, with how-
> ever, a jeweler's eye for political truths. . . .
> The jeweler knows value; that is his trade.[1]

What Buckley is talking about is discernment—the
jeweler's ability to distinguish one gem from another in
order to determine its true value. The jeweler differen-
tiates the spurious from the true and detects flaws and
imperfections not easily identified by other people.
As a political commentator, Buckley claims the same
ability in the realm of politics. Spiritual discernment is
similar, yet in one respect it is radically different.

The Christian's trade is *spiritual* discernment. You
would expect that in the most important area of one's

life he would seek to be as discerning as possible. Yet, as George Duncan has said, "It is a strange fact about life that many people who are careful and explicit and exact in almost every department of their lives are at the same time, when it comes to spiritual things, content with vague uncertainties."[2] Duncan is right. As we have seen, that is the situation today. We shall consider the reason behind this strange phenomenon in the next chapter. For now we must content ourselves with an understanding of the word and the biblical concept of discernment.

In the last chapter I said that spiritual discernment is the ability to distinguish God's thoughts and ways from all others. I shall stick by that definition while explaining what this means, adding certain thoughts that may not immediately be apparent, and giving examples of discernment in action.

Biblical Terminology

There are two principal terms in the Bible for discernment: the Hebrew word *bin* and the Greek *diakrino*. Both, in etymology and usage, are similar.

The Hebrew term *bin*, which is used 247 times in the Old Testament, has been translated in various ways—"understand, discern, distinguish." It is related to the noun *bayin*, which means "interval" or "space between," and the preposition *ben*, "between." In essence it means to separate things from one another at their points of difference in order to distinguish them. It refers to the process by which one comes to know or understand God's thoughts and ways through separating those things that differ. Discernment is skill in reaching understanding and knowledge by the use of a process of separation.

You can see how the concept of antithesis, of making a space between the thoughts and ways of God and of the world, is related to spiritual discernment. Also related is the idea of church discipline, by which space is made between the church and the world. The demise of systematic thought about the faith, along with the chaos of authority occasioned by the intemperate stampede of the laity into vying positions of self-assumed authority, weakens one's ability to discern the true from the false, the right from the wrong.

The Greek term used in the New Testament is similar to its Old Testament counterpart. *Diakrino* also means "to separate." The idea in this word is that through the use of separating discrimination a person makes judgments and decisions. It is used, for example, in Matthew 16:2,3 in reference to discriminating between different conditions of the sky in order to judge whether or not it will rain. Jesus uses this analogy to condemn the Pharisees for their inability to discern the signs of the times. Lack of spiritual discernment was a serious matter to our Lord.

In his book *The Struggle for Men's Hearts and Minds*, Charles Colson pictures the church today as "a church which increasingly accommodates secular values." He is speaking of a church that cannot (or will not) separate between those values which are taught in the Scriptures and those which are taught in the world. Integration by the accommodation of truth to error has brought about this condition. Such integration is the very opposite of the discriminating actions of persons with discernment. Colson's later admonition is to the point: *"We must discern the false values of this world—and reject them"* [emphasis his].[3]

Spiritual Discernment

Yet spiritual discernment differs from the kind of discernment that the jeweler possesses and political analysts like Buckley claim. The addition of the word "spiritual" is not merely a meaningless appendage or an adjective designed to distinguish the kind of discernment that is done by Christians from other kinds of discernment or the discernment of unbelievers—as if it meant no more than the word "Christian" now means. While the word "spiritual" certainly distinguishes the kind of discernment which believers have from all other kinds, there is a much larger reason for using it.

Spiritual discernment means just that: discernment that is given by the Spirit of God. In the next chapter we shall see exactly how the Spirit imparts discernment to His people, but for now it is enough simply to point out the vital fact that spiritual discernment is discernment given by the Spirit. Paul makes this perfectly clear in 1 Corinthians 2, where he speaks of the Spirit who dwells within the believer as the One who imparts the ability to ascertain the mind of God. The Spirit does this by enabling the regenerate person to successfully investigate the things of God in order to distinguish the wisdom of the world from the wisdom of God. This is spiritual discernment.

It is the necessary presence of the Spirit of God at work in the process, enlightening the believer so that he is able to understand the Scriptures, that makes spiritual discernment radically different from all other kinds of discernment. The jeweler's discernment differs from the political commentator's only in the subject treated and the methods appropriate to making distinctions crucial to each enterprise. Spiritual discernment differs from both in the same ways. But it also differs—and this iss what makes all the difference—beccause discernment of the will of God is not possible apart from the enlightening work of God's Spirit. In other words, God Himself, in a special way, is always involved in the process.

In defining spiritual discernment we may therefore say with a bit more precision that *it is the divinely given ability to distinguish God's thoughts and ways from all others.*

Examples of Discernment

Since we have seen that spiritual discernment is the Spirit-given ability to distinguish God's *thoughts* and God's *ways* from all others, let's look at an example of each.

Tony Walter has written an insightful (though sometimes disturbing book) titled *Need, The New Religion.* In it he shows plainly that the Maslow need theory—which holds that all human motivation results from need—is totally opposite to the Christian faith. Yet a majority of people today are attempting to interpret and live their lives according to this psychological theory. Walter says such penetrating things as this:

> People still work and bear and rear children, but the motive is no longer seen as purely of social or divine origin; it is believed increasingly to come from within. Less obligated to God or society, the free individual of modern democracies has invented a new obligation—to himself or herself. If duty is spoken of at all today, it is the duty to

oneself. . . . That inner needs now supple-
ment social norms and religious ethics shows
the essentially *moral* nature of psychological
needs . . . to abstain from [meeting] them is
immoral.[4]

Walter clearly discerns the great difference between
Maslow's need theory and the Christian faith. He does
not hesitate to set them forth in antithetical fashion in
his book, warning Christians of the dangers that lie in
the pathway of those who, in an undiscerning manner,
tread Maslow's pathway. The publication of such a
book today is unusual. It is rare to see insight, discernment and warning combined.[5]

Having cited an example of discernment in distinguishing God's thoughts from the world's, let us now
consider an example of distinguishing God's *ways* from
the world's way.

In 1987, according to the school newspaper, Biola
University's choir was scheduled to sing at Robert
Schuller's Crystal Cathedral. One choir member, to his
own detriment, refused to sing. He considered it his
duty to withdraw and lose his position in the choir, if
necessary, rather than to sing a version of Amazing
Grace that had been tinkered with to suit the self-
esteem doctrines of the church. Such discerning and
courageous action is all too seldom seen among Christian college students today. It was based upon proper
discernment of what was happening and led to a decision conforming to this young man's perception of the
facts. That was spiritual discernment in action!

Dangers to Avoid

In conclusion, I need to mention the fact that it
is possible to become so narrow in your concern for

purity and truth that you withdraw further and further into a shell. Perhaps the sad biographies of Arthur W. Pink best illustrate the extreme to which one can go. Increasingly unable to reach agreement with others, he first retreated from one continent to another, then from one congregation to another, finally leaving behind every church and living out the remainder of his days on an island in Scotland, where he and his wife worshiped at home alone. While few people will go so far as Pink, it is easy to see just how he reached this place. As you look around you, on every hand you see the great lack of discernment in the church. After trying to do something about it, you may come to believe that your efforts are useless—little more than a drop from a bucket. At that point it is tempting to cry out with Elijah, "I, I alone am left!"

But God didn't leave Elijah alone, and He hasn't left us alone, either. God has His thousands—perhaps this time even His millions! Those with spiritual discernment recognize this fact. I trust that you will not become discouraged as you undertake to separate those thoughts and ways that are God's from those that are not. Persist, and others will learn from you!

In all that you do, be absolutely sure that it is the biblically certain truths of God for which you contend. It is easy to identify one's own interpretations of the Bible with the Bible itself. Moreover, it is an equally fatal flaw in many people who mean well to confuse the traditions of the church with the teachings of Scripture. Spiritual discernment makes a person aware of such matters.

Discernment, the capacity to separate truth from error, is vitally important. The church cannot do without it. Apart from spiritual discernment it is impossible to determine and follow Romans 12:2: "Don't be conformed to the way of our modern age, but be transformed by the renewal of your mind, so that you may be able to determine what God's good and pleasing and perfect will is." Apart from following that will it is impossible to please Him.

As I stated in Chapter 2, in order to understand the current lack of discernment in the church and be able to do something about it, we must now look behind those proximate causes of the condition to the fundamental factor from which they all flow.

4

The Basic Problem

4

The Basic Problem

In a letter received by a friend, the writer says:

> A bank teller is not trained to catch coun-
> terfeit money. But handling the "real" and
> becoming acquainted with the "real," the
> moment a bad one comes across his hand he
> recognizes it.

He was speaking of discerning truth and error. His
idea is that when one becomes thoroughly familiar
with God's truth, he will automatically recognize Satan's counterfeit bills. Discernment of evil is the by-
product of learning to identify truth. We shall see that
there is a good deal to what he says.

Solomon's Discernment

Solomon was famed for his powers of discernment.
Solomon asked God for "an understanding [lit. "hearing"] heart" so that he could "judge" the people well by
being able "to discern [*bin*] between good and evil" (1
Kings 3:9). In response, we are told that God was
pleased with his request and gave him a discerning
heart (1 Kings 3:12). The text does not say how it was
given, but at first glance one might conclude that he

received it on the spot. The events that follow, beginning with verse 16, would seem to confirm the idea of a direct, immediate gift!

But a closer look throws some doubt on this idea. When God said, "I have given," He may only have *decreed* that Solomon would become discerning. God often speaks of what He has determined as if it were already accomplished. After all, what He has decreed is as good as done. As a matter of fact, in the very next verse He uses the same language and the same construction when He says "I *have* also *given* you . . . riches and honor," (1 Kings 3:13). Surely these did not appear immediately. Solomon's riches accumulated over a period of time and, as they did his fame also grew. Nor can anything be made of the transitional particle *az*, "then," in verse 16, in which we have the famous case of two women claiming to be the mother of the same child. *Az* can mean not only "at that time" but "after that" (at any time), or even "because of that." So it is altogether possible that, as with his riches and honor, Solomon's wisdom and powers of discernment were also acquired over a period of time. The evidence in the account does not allow one to be dogmatic on the point.

Either way, notice once more of what this discernment consisted: It was the *ability to distinguish good from evil* (1 Kings 3:9,11). In order to become a knowledgeable, wise judge of his people, discernment was necessary. Interestingly, the New Testament sets forth the very same understanding of discernment. In Hebrews 5:14 we read of "those whose faculties have been trained by practice to distinguish good from evil." Because this verse, and the passage with which it is connected, is so important to our discussion, we shall spend some time with it. Let me quote the entire passage so that we may consider the background of the verse:

> We have a lot to say about this, but it is hard to explain since you have become dull in hearing. Indeed, because of the length of time that has expired you ought to be teachers, yet you need someone to teach you the basic presuppositions of God's revelation once again. You need milk, not solid food. The truth is that everybody who feeds on milk is inexperienced with the righteous Word; he is still a baby. Solid food is for mature people, for those whose faculties have been trained by practice to distinguish good from evil (Hebrews 5:11-14).

Background

The writer of Hebrews was concerned about second-generation Jewish Christians who, at the first indications of persecution (none had been injured or martyred for his faith—Hebrews 12:4), were beginning to waver. This concern runs throughout the book as a dominant note. It seems that some were wondering whether it might be wiser to return to Judaism. They were possibly in danger of falling away from the faith. So the writer compares the Judaism which their fathers left with what they have received in Christ, and at all points shows how Christ is superior (the key word of the book is "better") to the types and shadows of Judaism.

In connection with one of his arguments, the writer had begun to speak about the priesthood of Christ.

There was much more that he would like to have said (Hebrews 5:11), but he found it difficult to do so. He hesitates in his argument to explain why. The difficulty is that he might find himself talking over his readers' heads. He shouldn't be—by now they ought to be able to teach others—but, sadly, because of their "dullness" he may very well find that they can't understand (verses 11,12). They are like babies that cannot eat solid food but still need milk (verse 12b-14a); they are "inexperienced with the righteous Word" (verse 13).

The readers of this church (or group of churches) had been drifting from the knowledge which their fathers had attained and had *become* dull in hearing. The word "become" indicates that there had been a retrogression, elsewhere called "falling away" (Hebrews 12:15), "throwing away of confidence" (10:35), "drawing back" (10:39) and "drifting away" (2:1). The problem lay primarily in the reader, not in the difficulty of the material the writer wishes to present; he attributes it to their "dullness in hearing." He fears that they might not be able to digest the solid food in the argument he wants to pursue. Their central problem was not persecution but a spiritual immaturity that caused them to waver in the face of persecution (Hebrews 5:12-14). Because of "dullness" the particulars of the Christian faith were not clear to them and so they were even able to entertain the possibility of returning to the "safer" Judaism of their fathers.

The problem is still with us. Like many second-generation Christians today, the original audience of the epistle to the Hebrews had lost their fathers' sense of antithesis. At the bottom of their problem was dullness in hearing the truth of God, due to lack of discernment, which in turn was the result of failure to regularly utilize the truth they *did* possess to distinguish truth from error so as to sharpen their powers of discernment. It is our problem as well. Let us examine each element of this problem as enunciated by the writer of Hebrews and see how it is with us today.

Dullness in Hearing

The kinds of things I talked about in the first chapter, those that are troubling and confusing the church today, would not get a hearing if there were not a similar widespread dullness in hearing.

The dullness of the Hebrews was in "hearing" they simply lacked the capacity to understand. Consequently they could not distinguish good from evil. They were easily taken in. Today people are exactly like that. Programs promising autographed pictures of Jesus Christ could not continue on the air if they were not supported by gullible Christians. Robert Schuller's "New Reformation" would be recognized for what it is—a move toward humanism in which man takes God's place—if Christians were not so dull in hearing. All kinds of cults and isms bordering on the cultic would not go far if Christians were spiritually mature, with faculties trained to discern between good and evil. But, as Paul put it by using two powerful metaphors, there are so many

> infants, blown about and carried around by every wind of teaching, by human trickery, by craftiness designed to lead to error (Ephesians 4:14).

Just what is this "dullness" (*nothros*) of which the author of Hebrews speaks? The word is a combination of two others: "no" plus "push" or "thrust." In the New Testament the word occurs only twice, here in Hebrews 5 and again in Hebrews 6:12, where it is translated "sluggish" or "dull." In the Old Testament, *nothros* appears only in Proverbs 22:29 of the Septuagint, where it refers to a person who is slothful in contrast to the diligent man. That is the fundamental idea inherent in the term: It means "one who is sluggish, indolent, lazy, or slow." *The Cambridge Greek Testament* translates "dull in hearing" as "lazy-eared." Dullness is also associated with illness. I have discovered one passage by Hippocrates, the famous Greek physician of antiquity, in which he describes a state of coma by using *nothros* in conjunction with *karosios*, which means "heaviness in the head."[1] The metaphorical use of *nothros* in Hebrews expresses the condition quite well: One is "spiritually unwell, encumbered by heaviness of head," or even in a coma-like condition spiritually.

Two things, therefore, may be said of the person who is *nothros*:

1. He is dull of apprehension. He lacks push and fails to move ahead on his own; he is not aggressive. There is a lack of eagerness and concern that causes him to dawdle. If this condition persists, he becomes lazy. If he will not sharpen his powers of discernment by aggressively practicing them, he will soon develop a lethargy and a habitual state of lazy nonchalance about the faith.

2. As it is used here and in 6:12, the term implies a state of culpable incapacity. As the writer indicates, the condition comes from the failure to take advantage of available truth by putting it to work in daily living.

Clement, bishop of Rome in the first century A.D., wrote:

> The good workman receives the bread of his labor with boldness, the lazy [*nothros*] and careless cannot look his employer in the face.[2]

In the next line, by contrast, Clement urges the reader to be "prompt" (or "eager, ready") to do good. The idea, then, is that the *nothros* person, by his failure to take advantage of his opportunities, has drifted into a state of lethargy, laziness, and unpreparedness in which he has become incapable of distinguishing between truth and error.

Training and Habit

All along I have found it necessary to allude to the fact that the dull readers fell into that state because of their failure to use rightly the faculties that they possessed. I do not mean to imply by the word "faculties" that there are some mechanical devices inside the Christian for making distinctions that, because of disuse, atrophied. The word used in Hebrews 5:14 for "faculties" or "senses" is *aistheterion*, the common Greek term for senses of perception (sight, hearing, touch, etc.). It is used that way throughout the writings of Diogenes Laertius, the historian who wrote about the lives of the great Greek philosophers. For example, when he discusses the teachings of various philosophers who dealt with sense perception he uses the same word that the writer of Hebrews uses to speak of the regenerate person's capacity to distinguish between God's truth and the devil's error. The writer is referring metaphorically to the inner life of the believer *as if* he had inner senses of perception that had to be trained to make distinctions as one's physical senses must.

A baby cannot discriminate sounds well so as to imitate them accurately. One of our children, for example, used to call pancakes, suitcases, and several other items "peebeeps." It took some input from us and some effort on her part to eventually sort out the concepts. Spiritual babies, dull in their hearing of truth, have similar problems in differentiating truth from error. One of the signs of growth in a child is the ability to discriminate. Before the development of discriminating powers, anything and everything goes into the mouth. Many immature Christians are like that: They will devour anything "religious," showing thereby their spiritual immaturity.

These spiritual babies are said to be "inexperienced" or "unskilled" (Hebrews 5:13). In contrast, those who are mature have senses (faculties) that are "exercised" or "trained by practice" so that they habitually discern between good and evil. The training mentioned in verse 14 is like the training of an athlete. The mature Christian, over a period of time, by making good distinctions and living in accordance with them, sharpens his senses to respond automatically or habitually to good and evil. He "develops a nose for truth," as we would say (ourselves referring metaphorically to the olfactory *sense*). He is a spiritual bank teller who has spent so much time handling God's truth that whenever counterfeit teaching passes through the fingers of his mind he immediately identifies it for what it is.

Both truth and error when accepted into thought, life, and ministry make an impression on the person.

Error dulls, leading the heart away from God, while truth sharpens him spiritually and in every other way.

The Word of Righteousness

The inexperience of these spiritual babies and their lack of training was given a specific focus by the writer of Hebrews: He calls them "inexperienced with the righteous Word." What does that mean? It can mean only one thing: the word of God that has to do with righteousness.[3]

The writer of Hebrews has already mentioned God's Word more than once; indeed, the epistle itself begins with the two ways that God spoke—in Old Testament times and at the beginning of New Testament times. He refers, of course, to the Old Testament prophets and to the person of Jesus Christ, whose message is now recorded in the books of the New Testament. The same two references to the Word appear also in Hebrews 2:1-4. There, as here, his concern is to get his readers to "pay attention to" that Word (2:1). And in the next chapter (6:5) he will speak once more of those who have "tasted the goodness of God's Word." Finally, they are urged to remember those who "spoke God's message" [lit. "word"] to them (13:7). In all of these instances, the reference is to the Word of God that had been recorded in the Old Testament and the words of Christ and the apostolic Word that has since that time come down to us as the New Testament.

It is called the "Word of *righteousness*" because it is at the same time the Standard of righteousness (i.e., the Standard against which to measure good and evil) and the Word through which a person becomes righteous (as by the Spirit's power he understands and obeys it).

In this passage the Word of righteousness is primarily considered the *Standard* of righteousness, since the writer's concern is discernment—the discrimination of righteousness from unrighteousness.

What the writer says is this: When one has reached the condition that is acquired by regular, disciplined practice in the discernment of good and evil, then (and only then) is he able to select the right way over the wrong.

Solomon asked God for "a hearing heart" (1 Kings 3:9)—a heart that will *listen* to God's Word, one that will understand and assent to God's Word and act accordingly.

Notice that the righteous man, who is experienced in discerning and living according to God's Word, is experienced in precisely *that*. It is not general experience that produces godly discernment, but only experience in *using God's Word to determine God's will*. In the Garden of Eden, Satan offered the knowledge of good and evil. That was an offer of knowledge by experience—gained the hard way. And it was set over against God's way of acquiring knowledge—by listening to His Word.

The distinction between learning from general experience or from the experience of following God's Word is of the utmost importance today. One way leads to dullness, the other to discernment. Everywhere Christians are writing about their experiences and teaching others how to live out of supposed "promptings and checks in the spirit." Yet nothing but the morass of subjectivity awaits those who follow this unbiblical route. It amounts to nothing more than an attempt to determine the will of God through the divination of feelings and circumstances. The Romans consulted chicken livers to learn the will of the gods, and Gypsies look at the configuration of tea leaves. But modern Christians smugly prefer the arrangement of circumstances and their inner hunches (usually called promptings). No wonder there is so little discernment! No wonder Christians are befuddled about doctrine and life! No wonder they muddle their way through decisions, and make so many poor ones! They do not know how to discern truth from error.

In 1 John 4:1 there is an exhortation to "test [the word for proving something to be genuine by means of testing] the spirits." As the passage continues, the test is applied to heretics in the early church who denied that Jesus Christ came in the flesh (verse 2,3). The test is doctrinal. There is no direction to consult your feelings about these persons or to expect any subjective promptings or checks. It is their *teaching* that must be examined. And, contrary to the understanding of those who superficially read the passage, the test for truth and error in every case is not whether people affirm or deny that Christ has come in the flesh. Many heretics believe He did. That was the specific doctrinal test that applied to *these* false teachers. The general test, of which this was but a particular example, is found in verse 6:

> Whoever knows God *listens to us*, but whoever isn't of God *doesn't listen to us*. From *this* we know the spirit of truth and the spirit of error.

There is no other test. Either someone's teaching matches the teaching of the apostles and the prophets (now found only in the Scriptures) or else it is false.

This was always the test. In Deuteronomy 13, where Moses warns of false teachers who would make predictions and claim to perform miracles, he explicitly tells us not to follow those teachers—*even if their predictions come to pass and miracles seem to occur*—if they proclaim a false God. Again, the standard is the teaching of the Scriptures: Is what they say about God scriptural? The test is doctrinal.

This exhortation is needed today, when all sorts of claims are made by leaders of every doctrinal stripe. Only consistent study of the Scriptures and the regular application of scriptural truth to the teachings of all who make such claims will sharpen one's discernment. Eventually, like the bank teller, he will be able to tell the good from the bad whenever and wherever he encounters it. The basic problem is that we have not been doing this or teaching people to do so. The solution is to begin doing it now.

5

Concern to Discern

5

Concern to Discern

So far we have observed several things: God holds us responsible for distinguishing between good and evil. When we are so dull that we make a hash out of that task, He is displeased, since He has given us all the resources necessary to discern truth. He expects us to rectify the situation (though I have not yet discussed how). Now I shall enlarge upon the last chapter, looking at what God says about discernment in other places in the Bible and learning from them additional aspects of the subject.

A Noble Task

I have alluded to the fact that there are those who consider discerning between good and evil a despicable activity, which they derisively label "heresy hunting." The mentality behind such language is dangerous. While sounding exceptionally pious, it discourages many inexperienced Christians from pursuing the God-given task of discriminating truth from falsehood and makes them easy marks for every sort of delusion.

Anti-heresy-hunters make a plea for "open-mindedness." I once studied under a professor who used to say, "Open minds are like open windows; you have to put in screens to keep the bugs out." The prudent believer screens every idea, every claim, every proposal, every opinion through the grid of Scripture. The Bible is his protection from the stings and bites of error. He is open to everything in the Bible, of course, but everything else must be examined carefully in the clear light of God's Word.

Is screening out error to determine what is true and false a disagreeable task such as, for example, cleaning toilets? Certainly not! While there are aspects of the two activities that bear a rough resemblance to each other, as a whole the task, though exacting, is wholesome and enjoyable. Every time a Christian scrubs away the filth and pollution of error, the truth shines ever more brightly, and he has the opportunity to affirm his allegiance to Christ afresh by choosing His way.

When Paul and Silas preached in Berea we are told that the Berean Jews

> received the Word with great eagerness, examining the Scriptures daily to see if these things were so. As a result, many of them believed (Acts 17:11,12a).

"Ah, there you have a pack of heresy hunters if there ever was one! Look at them pouncing on Paul and Silas' words, doubting their message and trying to find flaws in it. How dare they check up on the preaching of an apostle and his companion! Who do they think they are—unordained laymen—to search the Scriptures to see if the message is true?" That is how anti-heresy-hunters should react when reading this passage.

But that isn't the way Luke saw it. On the contrary, he strongly commends the Bereans: "Now these Jews were more noble than those in Thessalonica," he says, *because* they checked up on Paul to determine whether his message was biblical. And, he notes pointedly, "as a result, many of them believed."

The process of discernment—distinguishing truth from error by screening everything through the sieve of Scripture—is a *noble* activity. The next time someone calls you a "heresy hunter" when you are merely exercising discernment, screen *that* judgment biblically and you will discover not only that the charge has no substance but that the opposite is true.

What does God mean by declaring those who engage in distinguishing truth from error "noble"? The word is *eugenes*, meaning "wellborn, high-minded." Originally it described those who had been born into the artistocracy (Luke 19:12, 1 Corinthians 1:26). But, like the English word "noble," the term soon came to mean "noble-minded, high-minded, thinking and acting like a nobleman is supposed to act." Those who intensively work at searching the Scriptures regularly ("daily") to determine the truth or falsehood of a teaching are declared to be among God's nobility. Scripture searchers, far from being disparaged in the Bible, are said to be members of a spiritual aristocracy! Those who belittle the activity of discernment run the risk of lulling God's children into a state of spiritual dullness. They also contradict God when they do so.

Surely, if Luke commends those Jews who eagerly sought to find God's truth by using the Bible as their Standard for judging whether the teaching of Paul, an inspired apostle, was true, how much more important is it to evaluate what TV evangelists, writers of books (including this one), and other uninspired persons teach today! It is your privilege—even if you are a layman—to join the noble band of aristocratic Scripture searchers who, as a result, receive God's Word "with great eagerness."

I am aware of the fact that the Pharisees also searched the Scriptures (John 5:39) but did not believe. Plainly, then, not all searching is the same. The source which the Pharisees and the Bereans searched was identical, so the variables must be connected with the goal and manner of their searches. The Bereans looked to see if what Paul and Silas said was true; when they found it so, they believed. *They were searching for truth.* In contrast, the Pharisees were looking for error; they wanted to find passages to prove Christ wrong. They sought Scripture that would lend support to the traditions of the elders with which they had overlaid the Bible like a coat of thick paint, obscuring the beauty of truth beneath. Jesus said:

> You search the Scriptures because you think that by them you will gain eternal life. But they testify about Me! Yet you don't want to come to Me so that you will have life. . . . If you had believed Moses, you would have believed Me, because he wrote about Me. So if you don't believe his writings, how are you going to believe Me? (John 5:39,40,46,47).

Coming to the Scriptures for any purpose other than to discover and believe truth is contrary to and utterly defeats the discernment process. Through discernment, error is detected in order to enable a person to distinguish it from truth *so that he may learn and live by the truth.*

Test All Things

In 1 Thessalonians 5:21 Paul wrote, "Test all things and retain that which is good." Perhaps that translation is correct and the verse stands alone, as do verses 15-18, 25, 26 (which include commands such as "Always rejoice," "Pray regularly," and "Give thanks in every situation." On the other hand, it may be the continuation of an exhortation beginning in verse 20, which reads, "Don't dismiss the prophecies as if there were nothing to them," in which case the verse would be translated, "but test all of them [the prophecies] and retain those that are good."

Either way, the command stands: Test for the good, reject that which isn't, and retain that which is. All in all, this threefold command is as apt a description of the discernment process as can be found. In the one interpretation the process is focused upon a narrow issue; in the other it encompasses any and all circumstances in which discernment is called for. For our purposes, it doesn't really matter which view is right, since in both cases, the clearly described process is the same.

If verse 21 is a continuation of verse 20, as I tend to think it is, this only *strengthens* the point. If inspired prophecies in the apostolic age had to be subjected to testing (and of course that has always been necessary because of the prevalance of false prophets), then surely the teachings of uninspired men today should also be put to the test.

Of what does this testing consist? It involves evaluating the *content* of what is said in the light of Scripture. The prophecies were evaluated in order to determine whether they were true or false according to the teaching of the Bible. Such evaluation demands careful, active listening. That is why so many Christians fail; they prefer a more passive role. They either turn off most of what is said or else put the mind in neutral and let it coast with the speaker. Passive listening leads to spiritual dullness. Noble Christians will not settle for this. Their minds will be alive, actively comparing what is taught with the Word of God. They will test every new teaching to determine whether it is "good" (*kalos*, which means "worthy of acceptance").

The Christian faith demands much of the listener. It requires him to think, to be on the alert, to know his Bible well, to weigh and evaluate all that he is exposed to. God wants every member of His church to join the noble aristocracy of Scripture searchers. Jonathan Edwards, the great American preacher of the early 1700's, made this point very clear in his sermon on Hebrews 5:11-14. He said that every Christian who is sluggish and dull is condemned for not being able, instead, to *teach* the fundamentals of the faith. Again and again he drove home the point that knowing the Scriptures is the business not just of the clergy but of *every* Christian.

To "prove" or "test" (literally, to approve by testing) in 1 Thessalonians 5:21 means to assay content as a metallurgist does. It means to determine the genuineness of a preacher's or writer's coin. There is plenty of spiritual currency abroad, some genuine but much counterfeit. Every Christian, therefore, must so familiarize himself with the truth that he may readily distinguish between the spurious and the true.

The idea is not to pick at flaws or to have roast preacher for dinner each Sunday. The passage clearly states the object of the test: To identify that which is good so that you may "retain it." One must always search for more and more of God's truth for his own spiritual benefit and to pass on to others. The "good" is always one truth—God's way, while verse 22 makes it clear that there are many forms (species or kinds) of evil.

When discussing the biblical concept of antithesis, we saw that it is always God's way that is set over against all others. And in reality, though evil takes many forms, it too is one. Behind it one mastermind originates it all. Truth stands consistent with itself. Evil may take many, contradictory forms because none of them is true. The Scriptures are the touchstone against which all coins must be struck.

The Things That Are Worthwhile

Romans 2:18 and Philippians 1:10 are similar: In both verses the expression "determine the things that are worthwhile" appears. There is an alternate translation that is equally possible, for which many interpreters opt: "Distinguish the things that differ." Either translation leads us to the same destination. If one "distinguishes between things that differ" in a discerning way he will thereby "determine" those things that are "worthwhile." That is the natural result of the discernment process. On the other hand, if a person wants to "determine" those things that are "worthwhile," he must separate the things that differ: the good from the evil. He must exercise his power of discernment. For all practical purposes, when discussing discernment, there is little difference between the two translations.

The passage in Romans clearly designates the purpose for "determining the things that are worthwhile" (or "distinguishing the things that differ"): One does this to determine God's will. And, once again, we are told that the Standard by which such a determination or distinction is made is God's law (Scripture).

In Philippians 1:10 two additional items are mentioned: 1) Discernment is so important to the Christian life that Paul prays that the Philippians may have it; 2) this concern stems from the fact that God loves and cares for His children and knows that discernment will keep them free from impurities of doctrine and will eliminate many impediments that might hinder their spiritual growth. Paul wants your faith to be pure, free from all admixture[1] of false doctrine and practice, so that when Christ appears your life may be an honor to Him. That is precisely what the church needs today: to be freed from the humanistic, cultic, and otherwise unorthodox ideas and opinions that have been thoroughly stirred together with God's truth in an unholy amalgam.

Are you a member of the noble aristocracy of heresy hunters? Do you belong to that select band who can smell falsehood at 20 paces? Let this be true of you not because you are nasty and hard to get along with but because your search for truth requires you to peel off falsehood. Let it be true of you not because you love to criticize and find fault but because you really care about God's truth. Because you want to separate error from truth in your thinking and your living. Because you think it an impertinence to God for truth and error to remain together. Because you love Christ and want to serve Him in the purity and holiness of truth.

6

Learn to Discern

6

Learn to Discern

So far you have been exposed to a few samples of the kind of gullibility among Christians that cries out for discernment. You have seen something of why there is such a lack of discernment. You have learned that God requires discernment. But, until now, very little has been said about *how* you may become a discerning Christian. It is time to begin addressing that subject.

You Already Have Discernment

It is not as though you must start from scratch. Every Christian has some discernment, no matter how slight. If you believed the gospel—and you did, or you are not a Christian—you ought to be able to identify that message and distinguish it from false ideas of salvation. And, by virtue of reading this book, you have already begun to work on the problem. Perhaps even by now your awareness of the situation and the need for change has made you more conscious and alert in your thinking. If you have read in agreement up until now, you probably share a desire to become more discerning. Possibly you have begun to "see through" some of the wrong commitments into which you may have been duped. At the very least, you know what discernment is all about. You know that developing

79

spiritual discernment is an obligation before God. Indeed, by now you may be asking, "What must I do to grow more discerning?"

Perhaps you are thinking, "Is there hope for me?" From the way the writer of Hebrews portrayed the Jewish Christians to whom he was writing, you can only conclude that they too were in pretty bad shape. With every opportunity at their disposal (They had "once been enlightened . . . become sharers of the Holy Spirit . . . tasted the goodness of God's Word"— Hebrews 6:4,5) they did not grow as they should and remained spiritual infants. Yet the writer did not give up on them. True, his words in 5:11-14 are very sharp; he didn't excuse their condition. But those words were not intended mainly as a rebuke. Everything he said was calculated to awaken and stimulate them (and you). He was not trying to discourage them. This is apparent from the way he continues: ". . . we must advance toward maturity" (6:1). If there is hope for them, there is hope for you. And he does go on, providing more information and encouragement, warning and treating them as though he expected them to understand and respond. No matter how bad your condition today, if you are a genuine believer, the Spirit of God dwells in you, and that is all you need to begin to change.

Basically, it is the Spirit who, when you fervently ask Him, will lead you out of error into truth. He is called the "Spirit of truth" (John 14:17) because of His peculiar concern for imparting truth both by enabling its writers to produce an inerrant Bible (2 Peter 1:21) and enabling its readers to understand and apply its truth (1 John 2:27).

So, whether you have never made much progress at all, or you have grown lax in recent years (perhaps with a "What's the use?" attitude as you observe the massive confusion among believers), or you have never developed a regular program for growth in discernment, the encouragement in Hebrews is "Move on!" By God's grace you can do this. Now let's look at some principles that will enable you to exercise spiritual discernment.

Regularity

As we have seen, the capacity for discernment grows when it is regularly exercised. It is "by reason of use" that one's spiritual "faculties" become sensitive to the differences between truth and error. Spiritual discernment is a habit formed by using Scripture under the Spirit's power and direction to distinguish good from evil. Like any other habit of mind, it is established by regular, repetitive action.

At first, before any act, whether mental or physical, becomes habitual, it is difficult to perform. You feel awkward in attempting it. You do not perform it well, and the act must be done as the result of a conscious decision. But after much practice you perform skillfully, smoothly, unconsciously, automatically, and comfortably. It is merely a matter of getting over the hump. But this takes regular, daily effort in doing the right thing again and again over a period of time.

You probably remember how it was when you learned to drive. That first day, seated behind the wheel, you looked at the dials on the instrument panel, the gearshift lever, and the pedals on the floor, and you knew that somehow you had to learn to coordinate hands, feet, and eyes in order to drive. You wondered if you would ever succeed.

At first, with grinding gears, the car jerked unsteadily ahead and you recognized anew your total inability. You were unskilled. You felt awkward and had to make deliberate, conscious decisions about every motion. It was agony. But you had made a commitment, and you wanted very much to learn. So, in spite of discouragement, embarrassment, awkwardness, fear, and possibly even a dented fender or two, you persisted, you practiced, and—you learned!

Now, on a moonless night, in sheer darkness, you slide into the driver's seat, deftly slip a thin piece of metal into a narrow slot, turn on the engine, shift gears noiselessly, and drive off down the street. You haven't given the slightest thought to any of these actions; you did them skillfully, smoothly, automatically, unconsciously, and comfortably. All the while your mind could be occupied with some abstruse point of theology which you discuss with the person seated beside you.

How did you become so proficient? By committing yourself to the task. The same is true in developing any habit, including the habitual ability mentioned in Hebrews 5. You can learn to discern truth and error with the same or even greater proficiency if you will commit yourself to the task—and if you want it as badly.

The Necessary Commitment

Christians talk all the time about commitment, but rarely does anyone define it. I should like to mention five elements that are essential to genuine commitment. They are: knowledge, desire, capability, time, and effort. Let's look at each briefly.

1. *Knowledge*. If you don't understand what it is that you are committing yourself to, desire, capability, time, and effort won't do a bit of good. You simply must know what it is that you are getting into in order for any commitment to be fruitful. In this case it means having a pretty good idea of what discernment involves and what you must do to attain it. If you have read this far without putting the book aside, you should be aware of the former, and if you continue to read on to the end, you will learn about the latter.

2. *Desire*. You will need to look inside to determine whether you truly want to become discerning. I don't say that you must want to become discerning for discernment's sake. At bottom you must want it for Christ's sake. What is required is a desire to please Him. There will be obstacles in the way and periods of discouragement, so the desire—a desire at least equal to the desire that drove you to drive—must be present.

Many things that you do (take your wife out for dinner, for example) you may do not because you want to do them as such (you may prefer her home cooking) but to please another person (you know she needs a break and enjoys eating out). Much of what you must do to learn discernment is tedious (though it can also be exciting), and discernment may subject you to taunts that you have become a heresy hunter.

3. *Capability*. Often people fail right here. They know what is expected of them and they really want to do it, but they lack the resources and skills for bringing it off. Here is where you may founder if you are not careful. Resources are available, and later I shall suggest some. That it is possible to acquire the skills of discernment ought to be obvious, since you have already learned them to some extent and because you

have seen that God requires you to learn them. He requires nothing of His children that He doesn't provide all the resources and all the skills to accomplish—so long as they are willing to avail themselves of them. In the following chapters I have set forth a program for you to follow in order to get started.

4. *Time.* Unless you schedule a time, every day, to work on developing discernment skills, your good intentions will be worthless. You must state the exact time you will work on developing the requisite habits or else your desire, knowledge, and accumulation of resources will count for nothing. And don't tell me you don't have the time. Like everyone else, you have 24 hours a day. You must find the time. Naturally, you may have to eliminate other things. God gives each of us exactly enough time to do everything He wants us to do. We have only two problems: Finding out what He wants, and then doing it. Discernment is one thing He wants! And because it is a by-product of other activities, those activities must be done regularly—daily.

How much time is needed to follow this program? What is the best time to work at it? The answer to those questions will not be the same for everyone, but let me make a couple of suggestions that you may find helpful.

Developing a new pattern, we have seen, involves regularity. The best way to find time and achieve regularity is to hook your program onto something you do every day. Some of you may wish to study during the baby's nap, others early in the morning, and still others the last thing before going to bed. But one thing we all do is eat. Many Christians who take one hour for lunch—at work or at home—will find it helpful to devote half that lunchtime to eating (ordinarily you can eat lunch in half an hour) and half to practicing the principles of discernment. You should try several of these suggestions and discover which works best for you. Then stick to it until it becomes a vital part of your daily routine.

5. *Effort.* By this I mean that you must actually *expend* the effort. It does no good to schedule a beautiful program if you don't keep it. And if you keep it only sporadically, that won't work either. I'm talking about commitment. When you learned to drive, somehow or other you found the time and you regularly devoted yourself to the task of learning to drive, not missing an opportunity unless absolutely necessary. If you only will, *you can learn to discern*!

What Is Required?

Prayer is fundamental. Solomon prayed for discernment. Paul asked God for discernment for the Philippians. Underlying all else there must be a commitment to regularly ask God for discernment. You can go through all the motions according to the program in this book, but if God's Spirit isn't in it, permeating all you do *because you have asked Him to*, you will act in your own wisdom and strength and the result will be habits of sinful self-reliance. What you want are habits formed by the Spirit. The difference is seen in the attitudes and in the manner in which you will do what you do—whether you will become a Pharisee or the kind of Christian that God wants. Ask God to help you become discerning so that you will be able to uncover His truth as you should (not merely externally, like the Pharisees) and be able to apply it to your life and by this glorify God through helping many other people.

Bible study is essential. If you are honest, you will admit that you don't study your Bible half enough. Maybe you don't *study* your Bible at all! I'm not talking about reading the Bible; if you want to become discerning, you must learn to study it. If you don't know the difference, or how to go about it, then it's time to learn. You must study your Bible because it is the Standard against which you must measure all teaching. If you are not thoroughly familiar with your Yardstick, you will not be able to make good judgments about the things you are reading and hearing. Here I make two suggestions.

1. Probably your preacher would be delighted to teach a course in "How to Study Your Bible" if you asked him. Of course, you ought to interest at least a dozen or so others in the course beforehand. Perhaps by giving them a copy of this book you will be able to create interest.

2. If your pastor is unable to teach such a course, or needs a textbook for it, may I direct you to a book I wrote several years ago that was specifically designed to help people learn to *study* the Bible in a practical way. It is entitled *What to Do on Thursday* (Phillipsburg: Presbyterian and Reformed Publishing Co., 1982). It is possible to use that volume in conjunction with the program that I shall set forth in this book. The two would mesh nicely. So either independently or together with a small group of other people, learn how to study the Bible on your own. When you study the Bible you must study for facts, life, and ministry. Do not study, as so many wrongly do, for facts alone. Discernment is connected with all three.

a. *Facts.* Obviously, the more factual biblical data you acquire the more you will be able to distinguish truth from error. Remember the bank teller who, because he handles so much genuine currency, is able to immediately recognize the false? When you get the "feel" of truth—enough of it—you too will become adept in detecting error.

Suppose, for example, you hear a radio psychologist say, "God commands you to love yourself." This sounds suspicious to you. So you study the question in Scripture and you discover that no such command is ever given. The Bible presupposes that we already love ourselves far too much. The major concern is how to get us to love God and our neighbors. From your study you conclude that the psychologist is wrong. You are becoming more discerning. You will not pursue the fruitless and dangerous course of trying to love yourself more because you now realize that you have been exhorted by the Lord to love God and other people more. Your discernment is spiritually profitable.

b. *Life*. No truth should be studied in a vacuum (Deuteronomy 6:6ff.). It should always be learned for practical use and put to work in your life as soon as possible. Jesus gave the Great Commission in educational terms: "Teaching them to observe all that I have commanded you." Note the words "observe" and "commanded." His concern was not heads packed with facts for the next Bible quiz, but changed lives. The goal of the teaching was to transform the whole person, not merely accumulate data. (In *What to Do on Thursday* I have developed this point at length, so that a person using that textbook will learn how to transform truth into life.) The Bible comes to us not as an encyclopedia, with topics listed A-Z, but as *truth applied*. It teaches us what to do with truth—how to apply it to

daily living. The Bible is filled with Christ's command-
ments that He expects us to "observe," "do," "obey,"
and "keep."

Transforming truth into life helps one to discern.
If you have misinterpreted, misunderstood, or only
partly understood God's truth, when you try to apply it
you will find that it doesn't fit reality. In the attempt to
"observe" you will often discover that you need to
know more, that you did not quite get the right slant on
things, or that you wrongly understood from the first.
As far as discernment goes, application of truth to life
is a check to help you be more certain about the conclu-
sions you have reached in your study of the Bible.

Suppose you have read in a Christian magazine that
you should forgive others even if they fail to repent
of their sin (an unbiblical teaching that you will frequently encounter). You try it. But the one you "forgive" laughs at you and jumps all over you for suggest-
ing that there was anything to forgive in the first place.
You wonder why things went awry. This gesture on
your part was supposed to clear the air, but it didn't. So
you go back to Scripture and restudy the question
(perhaps consulting some books that will help you find
out what the biblical teaching is). You learn that you
must forgive in your heart, and hold no bitterness
against another person, but that you may *grant* forgiveness only when the other person professes repentance.
You cannot promise (forgiveness is essentially a promise) "I will remember your sins against you no more" if
in the future it is possible that God may require you to
raise the matter in obedience to His command to tell
one or two others, or even the whole church, in the
process of church discipline (Matthew 18:15ff.). So
failure to successfully utilize the idea (which in this

case you wrongly thought to be true) acted as a check, and drove you back to further study of the matter. Thus your discernment was sharpened by the incident.

c. *Ministry.* Ministry to others is the next goal of acquiring truth. You want to use what you have learned not for your own benefit alone, but also to help others. Because you have been blessed, you want others to share that blessing. You must never acquire truth merely for your own benefit. The Christian faith is no secret society that hides its knowledge esoterically behind the veil of some oath.

Even in this aspect, discernment grows. When you teach others by life (example) or by word, you recognize the fearful responsibility you have assumed. This alone should help you to become more conscientious in learning to discern truth lest you teach falsehood in God's name. Moreover, when teaching another person, questions often arise that you may never have thought to ask. In seeking answers to another person's questions you may learn more deeply yourself and may even be alerted to error you have unwittingly accepted as truth. You will find that Christ's aphorism "It is more blessed to give than to receive" holds true. And, though it is an old adage, let me repeat it nonetheless: The first time you know whether you really understand something is when you must teach it to another person.

Church participation is the third requirement. The ministry of the Word in preaching and in counseling was designed to help you become more discerning. Listen to Paul's words in Ephesians 4:11-14:

> He gave some as apostles, some as prophets, some as evangelists and some as shepherds

and teachers, to equip the saints for a work of service leading to the building up of Christ's body until we all attain to the unity of the faith and the full knowledge of God's Son, to mature manhood, to the point where we become as fully adult as Christ. This must happen so that we may no longer be infants, blown about and carried around by every wind of teaching, by human trickery, by craftiness designed to lead to error.

Notice that God has given officers to the church, especially the pastor-teacher, to prepare each member for his or her work of ministry. As I have indicated above, Christians must not learn truth selfishly, but must minister to others out of what they learn (Hebrews 10:24; Colossians 3:16; Ephesians 5:19). But many Christians are so unstable that they cannot help others; indeed, like babies, they need attention themselves. They are blown this way and that because they have no discernment.

Part of the problem is their own. Like the Hebrews, they have made it a habit to absent themselves from the preaching of the Word and from the mutual ministry of body members (Hebrews 10:25). The regular preaching of Scripture and its application to life will help willing believers become discerning. Moreover, the "one-anothering" activities in which all the members "stimulate one another to love and good works" has the same effect. So regular church attendance and full participation with the congregation is an essential factor in becoming a discerning Christian.

The problem also stems, in part, from poor preaching in which an adequate presentation of the biblical antithesis cannot be found. Lack of church discipline, psychological rather than biblical counseling, and a host of other pastoral deficiencies also account for the sad situation all around us today. But because I have already written much about these matters elsewhere, I shall not say more here except this: If your pastor has problems in these areas, pray for him, make it possible for him to attend seminars in which he can get help, and give him books that you think might be of benefit. Criticizing will help neither you nor him.

These three activities, then—prayer, Bible study, and church participation—are part of God's program for promoting discernment among His people. As you join in all three, you will soon discover your powers of discernment growing.

7

A Program

7

A Program

So you are committed to becoming a discerning Christian. You know what you are getting into, and you desire it for Christ's sake. You do not want to remain spiritually immature (you have noticed how often spiritual immaturity and lack of discernment are linked in the Bible). You want to develop the necessary skills, you plan to schedule time for this daily, and you will expend the effort. Though somewhat fearful of what lies ahead, nevertheless you are ready to move.

I do not say that the program I am about to suggest is the only way to become discerning. But it is *one* way. And, if you have no better, you might well adopt it. Of course, if you do adopt it, remember that you must not cut corners; you must not follow the program sporadically. If you do—don't expect results. Limited benefits may accrue to you through lesser efforts: consulting more than one Bible teacher, working with other people, etc. But even then, the regularity of disciplined daily work is the only way to develop new patterns of life.

When He told us how to be His disciples, Jesus said, "Take up [your] cross *daily* and follow Me" (Luke 9:23). The new life requires daily effort at crucifying self and affirming Him. The word used in Hebrews 5:14, *hexis*, means "habit, condition." The writer speaks of spiritual "senses" that had been habituated by the regular practice of distinguishing good from evil. This was because the readers had exercised these senses regularly. In speaking of the practice that led to that condition, he uses the term from which we get our word "gymnastics." It refers to athletic training, for which there are two absolute prerequisites: discipline (doing what you must, whether you feel like it or not) and regularity (not missing a day; sticking to your schedule). I emphasize these matters for two reasons: The text in Hebrews 5 makes a strong point of them, and it is in this area that most failure takes place.

I have tried to make this program as simple as possible. It consists of four elements:

1. Recording
2. Testing
3. Substituting
4. Implementing

To do this you need a looseleaf notebook set aside for this purpose. You will want to use a looseleaf notebook (or a card file of three-by-five cards if they can be carried more conveniently) because you may wish to add observations from time to time, and because it is best to arrange your entries alphabetically. We shall now examine each step of the program in order.

Recording

Recording consists of locating a problem (or possible problem) and stating in written form what was said, how it seemed problematic, and what you would like to know in order to investigate it further. It is really an effort to define the problem in clear terms to make sure that you understand it. Moreover, you will want before you at all times a concise statement of the problem on which you will be working. In that way you will not wander off into other matters. Much of our difficulty in learning to discern comes from not knowing precisely what we want to know.

1. Every day, without fail, record in your looseleaf notebook at least one statement, claim, or idea that you suspect *may* possibly be wrong or partly wrong. You may find material for recording:

    a. in books, magazines, newspapers
    b. on radio and TV shows
    c. at church in a Sunday school class, in sermons, or in conversations with other Christians.

At this stage, limit yourself to materials purporting to be Christian.

2. Allow an entire page for each entry.

3. At the top of the page, write one topic word that describes the area to which the matter pertains (e.g., Self-Esteem, Drugs, Sanctification, Marriage, etc.), perhaps with a subtopic (e.g., Drugs, withdrawal from).

4. On the next line write out the questionable statement, idea, claim, or opinion—*as you understand it, in your words*—in one sentence. This sentence will guide you throughout your study. You will refer back to it again and again; it is designed to focus your work and to keep you on track. So take care in formulating it. You may even want to refine and restate it until you are satisfied that it clearly identifies the issue.

5. In your one-sentence entry (when the material was orally delivered):

a. Capture the essence, or gist, of what was said.
b. Enclose in quotation marks any pithy three-to-five-word quotes that express the core of the problem content.
c. Beneath the one-sentence entry jot down any other supporting or clarifying facts that may help you in your study.

6. In your one-sentence entry (if the source is written material) summarize what was said, in your own words, and add any supporting or clarifying quotations from the article or book beneath the sentence itself.

7. Then write down all the questions to which you would like to have answers.

Let's look at an example. I am picking up the closest Christian book to me at the moment from a pile beside my desk. I am opening it at random and, as my eye scans the first page I look at, I read:

Studies have shown that many adolescents develop depressions after puberty. Their depressions result from a sort of mourning over the loss of childhood prerogatives. I think the same thing happens to many parents. They desire to go back to the time when they were free of responsibility.

I wonder about that, so I write:

DEPRESSION, Adolescents and

The claim is that adolescents and parents get depressed from "mourning" over the "loss of childhood prerogatives" that they had when "free of responsibility."

Note that I have a topic and subtopic, and a one-sentence statement of the questionable idea that I wish to examine.

Here are some observations and questions that I might write down:

Author claims that studies support idea of frequent adolescent depression after puberty, but cites no sources. Where did he get his facts? Were studies valid?

How does he know that depression results from mourning of the kind he claims?

What kind of theory lies behind his analysis of the facts (assuming the studies do show frequent depression after puberty)?

Note how he says he "thinks" something is true, but gives no reasons for thinking so.

Are there any biblical data to support such a reason for depression?

How does his notion square with data on depression in the Psalms and 2 Corinthians 4?

Is this mourning really depression or is he confusing things that differ?

What is this "mourning" like? He doesn't describe it.

Don't make entries of statements, ideas, and claims that you already know are right or wrong. The very fact that you will frequently encounter such material when working at this program should greatly encourage you. It means that you already *do* have some discernment and that your powers of discernment, though weak, are intact. They simply need exercise and expansion.

Here's another example which we will follow through.

On a Christian radio broadcast recently, the talk-show host advised a caller to "forgive God" when tragic things happen to her. You ought to recognize immediately that such advice is utterly erroneous. Did you? Well, the caller didn't, and you can be certain that hundreds of Christians listening soaked it up as a valuable new insight. The talk-show host offered no biblical support for his statement. If you are wondering about it, then this would be the kind of advice you might want to test biblically. Here's what you might write:

FORGIVENESS, Us to God

When tragic events strike our lives and we are wrestling with bitterness and anger, I am advised that I ought to "forgive God" for what happened.

Does the Bible ever tell me to forgive God?

Doesn't forgiving God imply that He did something wrong? If God can't do wrong, why should I forgive Him?

How does this teaching square with the promise that "God works all things together for my good"?

Testing

As we have seen, the Greek word *dokimazo* refers to approval or rejection on the basis of a test. In the New Testament we are told to "*test* the spirits to discover whether they are of God" (1 John 4:1-6), to "*discriminate* between things that differ" (Philippians 1:10), and to test everything carefully (1 Thessalonians 5:21). Elders and deacons must be tested before they take office; prophecies and teaching must be scrutinized; works and faith must be approved.

So testing is your second step. The key is knowing how to do the biblical study necessary to make proper evaluations of the issues you are testing. There isn't room here to do a detailed survey of this important issue, but let me make a few suggestions.

First, it is essential to know where to find the passages that address your questions. You must search the Scriptures to see if what you are wondering about is true. You need to take the questionable statement or claim and measure it by the biblical yardstick. Many Christians simply don't know their way around the Bible. To exercise discernment, it helps to know the major thrust or thrusts of each book of the Bible. In addition, it is important to know a number of the principal passages on various topics and themes. For example, could you quickly find some of the key New Testament passages on forgiveness? They would include Matthew 6:14,15 and 1 John 1:8-10.[1] The use of a concordance or Bible dictionary is also helpful in this process.

Assuming that you can locate the principal scriptural passages pertaining to your problem, there is also the need to properly interpret them. Generally, Christians tend to fail in this area in one of two ways: Either they depend entirely on the writings of others for help or else they lean totally on their own unaided understanding. What is needed is a proper balance between individual understanding and the help that others can give.

How does someone know the best meaning of a passage? Let me suggest four tools that will help.[2] First, examine the context of the word, verse, or passage. Second, observe similar usages by the same author, or in a similar context by some other writer. Third, use commentaries to see if there is general scholarly agreement or what the different interpretations are.[3] Last, use a variety of Bible translations; this is the easiest way to compare opinions on word usage. Every serious Bible student should have several translations available.

Now let's ask what passages might address this issue of "forgiving God." By use of the methods we've just briefly covered, we might list the following among many passages that shed light on our question:

> "Everything He does is great" (Mark 7:37).
> "Righteous and genuine are Your ways. . . .
> Your righteous acts have been manifested"
> (Revelation 15:3,4).
> "[God] is not a man that He should change
> His mind" (1 Samuel 15:29).

How would you go about evaluating the talk-show host's statement in the light of such verses? Write out your answer:

_____

_____

_____

_____

_____

Not every Scripture passage you find necessarily merits equal consideration in testing a claim. You need to study each in light of its context. You should consult commentaries to be sure you are interpreting it correctly. You might find that one passage is more to the point for testing the claim than the others. Would you consider one of the above three Scripture portions more to the point than the others? If so, why?

Having answered any such questions that arise, on the page of your looseleaf notebook you should now:

1. List the verses you found pertinent, and eliminate any verses (after careful consideration and study) that seemed not to be so.

2. Write out in one sentence what you found right or wrong biblically about the claim. Then, if necessary, in one paragraph write out any reasoning from Scripture to your conclusion that you may want to remember later on.

Substituting

Substituting the biblical alternative for the claim that was tested is pertinent only in those cases where the claim failed to pass muster biblically. Simply omit this third step and go on to the next when the claims hold up.

1. If the claim proved unbiblical, you must now look for the biblical alternative. It is important to reject what is wrong, but it is even more important to determine what is right. You should be searching for *truth* when you search the Scriptures. You have already invested time and interest in the matter. Now you should attempt to determine what God *does* say.

2. This may not always be easy. Often it is easier to discover what is wrong than to decide what is right. That's why the wrong kind of heresy hunting is so prevalent. Persist. If, after giving suitable time and attention to the matter, you cannot arrive at the biblical alternative, leave a blank and indicate this fact by a noticeable mark flagging the page, so that you will be reminded whenever you open the notebook that there is unfinished work to be done. Never settle for guesswork. From time to time come back to the problem. Eventually you will be able to eliminate the flag.

3. When you discover the biblical alternative, write it out in one sentence.

4. Then, under that sentence, in a paragraph or two, explain anything that is not altogether clear, amplify your statement, and (for the benefit of future reference) sketch the process of study and reasoning from pertinent Scripture that led you to your conclusion.

Regarding your evaluation of "Forgive God," what would be the substitute? Among the many passages available, you might consider the following verses:

"Consider it entirely a happy situation when you fall into trials of various sorts" (James 1:2).

"Always rejoice. Pray regularly. Give thanks in every situation; this is God's will for you in Christ Jesus" (1 Thessalonians 5:16-18).

In light of these verses, what would you recommend to that caller instead of what the talk-show host said? Write out your answer:

_____
_____
_____
_____
_____

Implementing

As the last step you want to ask:

1. How can I put this biblical truth to work in my life?
2. How can I help others to do so as well?

Do not answer these two questions with generalizations. Be specific and concrete. Think of actual situations in which you and others are involved to which the biblical truth might apply; then prepare to apply the truth to those situations.

The process of implementation is the *practical application* of biblical truth for biblical purposes, according to a biblically derived *plan* and *schedule*, together with biblical or biblically legitimate methods for meeting the schedule. Implementation has to do with *works*. The apostles Paul and James both taught that true faith always leads to works that are pleasing to God. It is never enough for us to know the facts of the Bible to the exclusion of ways and means.[4]

State in writing on your page exactly what you intend to do, when you intend to begin (use an exact date), and how you envision doing so. Never fail to do all three of these things.

Once more, let's return to the advice given by the talk-show host. We have determined that his teaching cannot be supported biblically. We have substituted the truth as revealed in Scripture. Now, do you have a situation where you can apply the truth you have just learned? If so, write it down here:

Is there someone you know who has a problem, like the caller to the talk show, to which this truth would apply? Write the first name of the person and the problem here:

Now choose one of the above and answer the following questions:

1. In light of the truth of Scripture that I've just observed, I plan to:

_____

_____

2. I plan to do this (state exact date and time):

_____

3. Here is how I will implement this plan:

_____

_____

What Next?

What should you do now? Well, of course, implement the truth according to your program. But I suggest that you also do the following: Sit down every Sunday for half an hour to an hour and reread your entries for the week. You may wish to add to earlier comments, revise others, and even (in rare instances) do one of them all over again. Getting some perspective on work that is well done but not fully mature may be the most important thing you do. You may want to check up on your implementation of the truth. Have you run into difficulties? What are they? How may they be overcome? Was your immediate goal too ambitious? You may wish to record any results. Having finished all this, you will then want to arrange the week's pages in alphabetical order according to their topic headings.

Next, ask yourself, "Am I becoming more discerning? Do I think things through more, even when I am not actively attempting to do so?" In six weeks of proper, disciplined, regular effort you should be noticing a difference. In six months (and you can abandon the formal program then if you want to) you should notice large gains.

To spur you on in times of discouragement or difficulty, let me give you a Proverb that may encourage you to persist:

> The naive believes everything, but the prudent man considers his steps (Proverbs 14:15).

Now let's examine one other very important issue as it relates to discernment. It is one that affects you in some way every single day. It has to do with your money, and the numerous appeals you receive for giving. It is an area that definitely requires discernment.

8

Discernment in Giving

8

Discernment in Giving

This book was already in the publisher's hands when the Jim Bakker/Oral Roberts events (already referred to) occurred. Because these events were placarded across the news media it seems highly appropriate to consider a couple of issues relating to discernment, and its lack, that have now surfaced.

Stewardship

Our money is not really our own. As the parables of the talents make clear, all that we have has been given to us by God as a trust to be used for Him. This does not mean that we can never enjoy anything ourselves: 1 Timothy 6:17 teaches that "God . . . richly provides everything for our enjoyment." So long as our money is used responsibly in a way that honors God we may enjoy its use. However, the money we *give* as well as the money we *spend* must be used with care and according to biblical principles.

That is why, when Paul collected money for the relief of the poor Christians at Jerusalem, he took meticulous care to make sure that every cent was spent according to the purpose for which it was given. And he assured the churches which gave that every detail of this collection was above reproach. Here is what he wrote:

Thanks be to God for putting the same earnest concern for you in Titus' heart, because he welcomed our appeal and has such earnest concern for you that he is coming to you on his own accord.

And together with him we are sending the brother who is well thought of throughout all the churches for his part in the furthering of the good news.

And not only that, but he also has been selected by the churches to accompany us in the gathering of this charitable collection in which we are serving as administrators for the Lord's own glory and to show our eagerness.

What we want to avoid is for anyone to be able to criticize the service that we are rendering in collecting this abundant gift, so we plan ahead to do good not only in the Lord's sight, but also in the sight of people (2 Corinthians 8:16-21).

First, Paul certifies Titus as trustworthy, and then he mentions another unnamed brother (8:18) "who is well thought of throughout all the churches" and "has been selected by the churches." Paul made sure that every giving church took responsibility for the distribution of the funds and had a way of determining that the money was used properly. He says:

What we want to avoid is for anyone to be able to criticize . . . (8:20).

Paul was aware that when it comes to fund-raising, improprieties are rife and misunderstandings can easily arise. So he said:

We plan ahead to do good not only in the Lord's sight, but also in the sight of people (8:21).

He was not only concerned about doing right, but he also recognized the importance of appearing right. He also assured his readers:

As for Titus, he is my partner and co-worker in serving you; as for our brothers, they are delegates from the churches, appointed to see that Christ is glorified (8:23).

Here he indicates that part of the plan by which the churches could know that their money was going to be used rightly was asking them to elect delegates as their representatives to go along with the gift.

Out of this passage, note at least these points:

1. Paul was aware of the potential problems associated with fund-raising and took concrete measures to assure givers that their money would be used for the purposes for which it was given.

2. He asked giving churches to select representatives to accompany the funds to their destination so that, having delegates on the spot, they could see to it that the funds were distributed properly.

3. The churches, as churches, were involved in the giving-and-evaluating process. Accountability was put into the hands of the churches as official bodies.

4. Paul carefully planned all this ahead of time so that from the outset, before anyone gave, all would know that there was no hanky-panky involved. He took pre-caution.

Out of the analysis of the passage two significant principles arise:

First, *the one soliciting funds* is responsible to provide a preplanned method for assuring givers that all is aboveboard.

Second, *the one giving* is responsible to take measures to see that the Lord's money distributed by him is used properly.

This means that the one soliciting funds should be concerned and careful how he collects funds. Before asking for them, he should plan workable ways and means to assure givers that their funds will be used as he claims. It is safe to say that any person or group that provides no way of making known where its money is going should be suspect and probably you should withhold your financial support until it provides disclosure.

On the other hand, the giver is responsible to see to it that the Lord's money, over which he has stewardship, is spent properly. He may ask for financial statements from the ministry seeking his funds. Another way to determine whether you should give to any cause is to ask your church. Notice how Paul brought the churches, as churches, into his giving program. Too often Christians give without the knowledge or wisdom that their churches could provide.

It is part of the responsibility of the leaders of your church to advise you about giving, and it is their responsibility to know about the beliefs and the activities of various organizations that solicit funds. If neither you nor they know about a particular ministry, they can help you find out.

In other words, God places responsibility on both sides of the giving/receiving transaction. He expects us to use discernment in giving, just as He expects those who solicit funds from us to use discernment in asking.

The Glory of Christ

In 2 Corinthians 8:23 Paul expresses his concern for the "glory of Christ," which is the ultimate purpose for all giving. We should not give merely to help the poor—the world does that—but *to honor God by giving to the poor*. The churches appointed delegates to accompany funds not from selfish motives, or even from mere humanitarian ones, but to be sure that their giving truly honored Christ.

Few things tarnish Christ's name before the world more than a scandal about money. That is why the Bakker scandal and Roberts' method of appeal are so tragic!

But they are not the only ones who disgrace the Lord's name by their methods. A current practice in appealing for money is to employ computers to send what purports to be a *personal* letter that sounds like the solicitor is actually thinking or praying about each individual. Consider the following, for example, from a television preacher:

> Dear Brother [recipient's last name],
>
> The Lord showed me how, there in [recipient's city] you can "feel" His "resurrection power"—like never before—during this Easter Season.
>
> As I was praying that God would meet all the needs in your life, the Lord led me to anoint the enclosed "Easter Cross Prayer Cloth" with oil and send it to you there in [recipient's city].
>
> Brother [name], please "peel" this anointed cloth and wear it on your lapel—or—collar

through Easter. I believe you will feel the assurance of my prayers for you that God will meet all the needs in your life.

God spoke to me that He will use this anointed "Easter Cross Prayer Cloth" just like He used Paul's, in Acts 19:11-12.

Brother [name], search your heart and think of any prayer needs that you have in your life. Then . . . after peeling off your Cross Prayer Cloth from the enclosed golden prayer card, write them down, in the name of Jesus, and return them to me immediately, so I will know *how* to pray!

Brother [name], I believe God has put you and I together for a purpose. We're not independent of each other. From the time you first wrote me, I knew that you were dependent upon my prayers to touch God for you, and I am dependent on your prayers and support for this ministry.

Apart from obvious grammatical affronts, consider this letter. The recipient's name is used throughout, as though this were a personal letter. Yes, *Reader's Digest* does the same, but Christian ethics aren't derived from what the world does! But the letter goes further; the potential giver is to write down prayer needs so that the solicitor, speaking in the first person, "will know *how* to pray"! Come on now! How gullible can one be? Do you really suppose he will look through every request and pray personally for it? You know better. Or do you? Evidently thousands of Christians who keep this ministry going can't see through it—or willingly go along with it and send in their money. Is Christ honored by such methods?

The same connection between Christ's honor and the giving of money is found in 3 John 7,8, where the apostle John makes it plain that funds to support the Lord's work should be solicited only from believers (as Paul did), and not from the world in general, for the sake of Christ's name. Here is another index by which you can determine whether to support any given ministry or not: To whom is the appeal for funds made?

Today some TV evangelists not only appeal to all listeners in general, but even bring on their programs movie and TV celebrities whose profession of faith is highly questionable, given their style of life and their comments elsewhere. Such methods surely should make one cautious about supporting the "ministry."

Lack of discernment is at the root of the scandals and the consequent loss of money to the church and other truly worthy Christian causes. But of greater importance, the church and her Lord are made the butt of the world's scorn. Once again, the solution to this problem is *discernment* (the ability to distinguish worthy from unworthy causes) through the knowledge and application of biblical teaching regarding stewardship.

9

Some Trial Materials

9

Some Trial Materials

In this chapter you will find material that may be used in class, on your own, or in a small group. They are statements I have read or heard from Christians in preaching, teaching, or casual conversation. Read over these samples, considering each item. Check those of which you are suspicious. Then, in your looseleaf notebook, treat these checked items as I have suggested in Chapter 7. Utilize the full process. Not every item contains material that is necessarily wrong. Remember, you are looking for *truth*. You will find it when you are able to identify truth for what it is, to eliminate any error that is present, and to match the remainder with scriptural teaching. Enjoy your work!

1. The fundamental purpose of marriage is procreation. That is why two persons who consent to sexual relations outside of a formal contract of marriage are nevertheless married in God's sight.

2. It is always incumbent upon the person who has offended another person to go to him and seek his forgiveness, but there is no obligation on the part of the one who has been offended to seek reconciliation.

3. When a man leaves his father and mother, and cleaves to a wife, he becomes the head of a new

decision-making unit that is totally independent of his parents.

4. The most important task which a Christian has to perform in this world is to change those structures in society and in government that do not agree with God's Word.

5. Cremation is every bit as valid as burial.

6. I'm so thankful that God made it clear to me that my prayer life was all wrong. I now know that I must "pray without ceasing." I haven't been able to pray about everything I do yet, but I'm working on it. It's difficult to remember to pray about the selection of each tie, shirt, etc., but the day may come when I really do it.

7. It's all right to be angry with God. What He is concerned about is honest openness on your part. Tell Him off. Make it clear just how you feel. The important thing is to express your feelings fully.

8. The Bible never tells us to endeavor to have a good self-image; the biblical concern is for us to have an accurate self-image.

9. A pastor's task is to evangelize his neighborhood. I simply can't understand why pastors are involved in so many other matters that keep them from their main work. They should be out there knocking on doors, preaching evangelistic services, and holding evangelistic Bible studies. No wonder our churches don't grow.

10. What we need is less head knowledge and more heart knowledge.

11. If a person is heading in the right direction, he will have "peace" about what he is doing. That is what Paul teaches in Colossians 3:15.

12. God hates the sin but loves the sinner.

13. If Christians don't support their church it will not grow. Every person should be there whenever the doors are open, unless it is utterly impossible for him to do so.

14. Because our God is a covenant God who works with families, it is important for the entire family to be present, sitting together on the pew. This demonstrates the solidarity of the family before God. Putting children in nurseries or in special meetings designed for them only destroys the family and destroys our testimony to God's covenant faithfulness.

15. Sure, the Bible has everything we need to know about church life, but it certainly doesn't tell us everything we need to know to get along with other people in this complex, modern world.

16. God wants you to be concerned about how you communicate with your children. If your words are mainly put-downs, if your gestures and facial expressions send mainly negative messages, you will warp your child's personality for life. It is a precious, tender, impressionable little being you have to train, and you must do so with the utmost precaution and care.

17. Forgiveness is not forgiveness unless there is forgetting. If you don't forgive and forget, God will still hold you responsible.

18. First you must get your feeling in line. If you go ahead and obey a command merely because the Bible directs you to do so, but you do not feel like doing it, you will be a hypocrite. God wants genuine, willing obedience from His children.

19. A person should obey God whether he feels like it or not because he wants to please God.

20. What a grand truth it is! The Spirit dwells within, guiding and leading us. How difficult it would be if we had only the Bible to tell us what to do; after all, the Bible says nothing about many of the decisions that we modern Christians must make every day. Thank God for the leading of the Spirit.

21. Sports programs are ruining our Christian schools. I'm not talking about all the unnecessary injuries and expenses to families that are incurred as a result of such programs, but about the fact that athletic contests are pagan. Christians should not be pitted against one another as rivals. There is enough pride and rivalry in the human heart already. What a disgrace to attend functions conducted by Christians and hear parents shout, "Kill the bum!" and players boast, "We're number one!" Let's do away with this pagan activity. Sports has become the American religion. Why should Christians propagate it?

22. If God is sovereign and determines what I will do, then He will not hold me responsible for my actions. After all, what else could I do?

23. Jesus and the apostles either bought into the common beliefs of the day about demons or accommodated themselves to them. Today we know that what primitive people thought of as demonic influence was really various forms of mental illness.

24. The Old Testament has no authority over us today. Only the New Testament guides us in daily living.

25. Healing of the memories is a foolish concept. Memories don't become ill! Moreover, there isn't the slightest whisper about any such activity in the Bible. In many cases, this procedure becomes an inadequate

and unbiblical substitute for biblical forgiveness and reconciliation.

26. It is always wrong to be angry. Man's anger doesn't work the righteousness of God.

27. There are two kinds of doubt. One is condemned by the Bible and the other is not.

28. God says that "love covers a multitude of sins." This means that God doesn't want you rebuking others for their sins and seeking forgiveness. Love is all that is necessary. Where love is, all these other things, right enough in their place, are unnecessary.

29. Church discipline is not possible in our modern world. It is a relic of the past that ought not be revived.

30. Of course wives should submit to their husbands, but husbands should submit to their wives also. After all, the Bible tells us all to submit "to one another."

31. All sins are not alike. God hates some sins more than others.

32. Sins may be forgiven, but this doesn't mean that all the consequences of those sins will automatically be erased as well, does it?

33. Now that I have become a Christian, I don't have to turn myself in for committing the crime.

34. There is no way to make restitution if the person to whom restitution is due has died.

35. Oral sex is forbidden in the Bible.

36. AIDS is a plain and unmistakable judgment of God on sin. Like any other sin, the tragic fact is that others not implicated in it may be detrimentally affected by it.

37. The unpardonable sin is saying no to the gospel. Whenever anyone does that, there is no sense in witnessing to him again. He is beyond hope.

38. If my wife were to submit to me, then I could be the head of my home. After all, how can I lead unless she follows?

39. The Bible instructs us to "heap coals of fire" on the heads of our enemies. That means that I can do good to him as a means of vindicating myself and getting even with him. It is comforting to know that the Bible has such a realistic approach to interpersonal relationships.

40. Since God commands me to obey the government, whenever the government tells me to do something which involves violating some other commandment of God, I may in that instance violate God's command if it is not so broad and basic as the former one.

41. All of life is religious. There is therefore no such thing as the secular. What we are talking about is the way in which unbelievers think about life; Christians should consider every area of life sacred to God. It is His creation and exists for His glory.

42. "Excommunication" is a word not found in the Bible. The idea is medieval and grew out of the Roman Catholic tradition. Protestants should never use the word and certainly should not practice it.

43. Until my basic needs have been met, I cannot become a self-actualized person, reaching out to others, loving God and my neighbor.

44. God wants us to grow up into mature persons who do not depend on others. Autonomy, the greatest sign of maturity, is the goal He sets for all His children.

45. Since the reason why God placed us here is to make us happy, it is certain that whatever restricts or prohibits happiness is in some way or other wrong and

must be eliminated from the picture.

46. God is the God of health and wholeness. None of His children, therefore, ought to get sick. When they do, as of course they sometimes do, it is because in some way or other they have failed to live according to His Word.

47. On the whole, Christians will be healthier, richer, happier, and better adjusted than others. All the great artistic, scientific, and other significant movements that have occurred in this world were in one way or another sparked by Christians.

48. The Bible commands, "Owe no man anything." This means that until he has saved up all the money to buy it, no Christian may purchase a home. Time payments, borrowing, and the like not only get us into financial trouble but are evidence of disobedience to Scripture.

49. The oldest child is always in danger of special peril and temptation, as numerous Old Testament stories plainly indicate. If, therefore, you are a firstborn, you had better learn all the Bible has to say about the dangers inherent in that position.

50. The exact words of a passage of Scripture are not all that important. What counts is the idea; it is ideas, not the words, that are inspired.

The preceding samples have been singled out for you, making the problems easier to identify. When you are reading along or listening to a speaker, such doubt-causing statements may tend to recede into the background or blend themselves with the maze of words. However, as you grow in discernment, more and more you will find that they stand out as vividly as if they had been abstracted from the whole and placed by themselves the way these statements have. When that begins to happen, you will know that you are making progress. You will be laying the counterfeit bills aside as a matter of course.

10

Conclusion

10

Conclusion

You are to be commended for sticking it out! Not everyone who purchased this book did so. Some laid it aside as a good idea to be pursued later. Probably a few of them will, but only a few. What you don't do at the moment when you are hot on doing it isn't likely to get done at all. The pressures and demands of our life-styles are too great.

There are other people, unlike you, who have read the first several chapters up to the proposed program and were interested and perhaps even intrigued. But when it got down to a commitment, and as they scanned the program, they decided that it looked like too much work. If I could have suggested some way to attain instant discernment, preferably to be infused into them at 2 A.M. on Friday while they sleep, they would have gone for it like a trout for his favorite lure. But to devote time, effort, and regular work to this project? That's asking too much. They are and will remain *nothros*—unless the Lord graciously stirs them by some tragedy, either to themselves or to a member of their family, arising out of their failure to take the matter of discernment seriously.

Count the True Cost

There are those who, having recognized the problem and their own inadequacy, have begun right away and are already plowing ahead, making slow but steady progress. Perhaps you will soon be among these people.

On the other hand, perhaps you are like a great number of those who have gotten this far: You are wavering, hesitating, wondering whether you really ought to commit yourself to this program. Good! You are counting the cost. But be sure to count not only what it will cost you to become discerning; count also the cost of *not* growing in discernment. I urge you to think of some of the consequences of not being able to distinguish good from evil. I won't list them; think for yourself. Also think of what it means in your relationship to the Lord. It is one thing to slumber along in immaturity as a Christian who doesn't know any better—that's bad enough. But now you have read this book, and you do know better. You know what God requires of you, and in your hand you hold the means of achieving it. There is no reason for putting it off.

I know all the excuses you might give relating to time. But you know as well as I do that what you really *want* to do you find the time to do. The Lord will help you make time. Talk to Him about the matter and begin to clear away some daily time for pursuing your growth in discernment. For starters, you could eliminate one TV program a day.

And speaking of starters, let me make a suggestion. Why don't you test the program for about two months, working on the items in the last chapter on Monday through Friday and adding items of your own on Saturdays and Sundays? That would give you a pretty good idea of what it will be like for the following four months. (Remember, this is a six-month program at the minimum.)

My Plea

I am pleading with you for the sake of the entire church. There is every reason to expect a period of great conflict with the pagan forces of society in the not-too-distant future. The church must be prepared. Humanism—the belief that puts man in God's place— has never been so outspoken, so powerful, and so bent on destroying the church. Humanists hold the key posts in society. There have already been numerous clashes over issues such as Christian schools, homosexuality, and abortion in which Christians have not come off all that well. One of the major reasons why the potential power of Christianity is not unleashed to wipe humanistic plans off the drawing boards is because of the woeful inability of so many Christians to discern. They accept humanistic teaching, thinly disguised as "scientific fact," "Christian principles," and the like, as it appears in Christian publications and as it is propagated unwittingly over Christian radio and TV programs. It is time we awakened from our slumber to see that a daily diet of humanism certainly won't help us to combat humanism!

Your children and mine will be affected by what you, and others like you, do. Will you become part of the solution rather than remain a part of the problem? Will you do all you can to become discerning and to encourage your Christian friends and your family to do the same? If you do, the next generation will inherit both a church and a country that is much more aware

134 • A Call to Discernment

of and obedient to God's truth rather than one that is wholly taken over by humanism. Which do you want for your children?

But, most important of all, God is grieved with immaturity in Christians who ought to be adult in their understanding. His command to you, if you are among those who need to hear it, is "Grow up!"

A Sobering Parable

To close this book, I give you this parable. Two men sat down before the TV to watch. The one was a man of discernment, the other was not. The televangelist said, "If you listen to my words and send me money, you and your family will prosper and remain healthy. If any should be hurt or get sick, he will surely be healed. Follow me." The former listened and wondered. He doubted what he heard and searched the Scriptures to see whether these things were so. As a result he rejected what he heard.

The other Christian swallowed every word. After a time the discerning man's son became very ill. The simple man's son also became ill. The discerning man took his son to the hospital and prayed that the doctors and nurses would be used by God to restore him. In time he was raised up and restored to health. The simple man trusted the televangelist and prayed, but did not take his son to the hospital, saying, "Surely the Lord will bless my faith." But in time his son became worse and died.

Let him who thinketh he standeth take heed lest he fall—through lack of discernment!

Notes

Notes

Chapter 1—The Lack of Spiritual Discernment
1. "TV's Unholy Row," in *Time*, Apr. 6, 1987, p. 60.

Chapter 2—What Caused This Lack?
1. For a thorough study of church discipline, see my *Handbook of Church Discipline* (Grand Rapids: Zondervan, 1986).
2. So-called Values Clarification programs, for example, are designed to destroy antithetical thinking and to inculcate continuum thinking. In one widely used textbook the purpose of one strategy is described as follows: "Students begin to realize that on most issues there are many shades of gray, and they are more likely to move away from the either-or, black-white thinking which often occurs. . . . This is an excellent strategy to use when you sense the class is thinking very narrowly. . . ." From Simon, Howe, and Kisschenbaum, *Values Clarification* (New York: Hart Publishing Co., 1972), pp. 116, 129.
3. In an open letter of Oct. 20, 1986, from Ronald Enroth, Professor of Sociology at Westmont College, Santa Barbara, California.
4. Ibid.
5. It is important to know how to distinguish a scriptural system from one that purports to be but is not. A nonscriptural system is built out of nonbiblical lumber. It is still nonscriptural, regardless of how many verses are stuffed into the pigeonholes of the system. A truly scriptural system is built out of biblical lumber, according to biblical blueprints (presuppositions and principles), and in biblical ways. Too many counseling systems that claim to be Christian or biblical are anything but, even

though they employ a lot of biblical terminology and refer to biblical content. The problem is that the system is based on Adler, Maslow, Ellis, Jung, Rogers, or some other psychologist's views and the Bible is only used to support it (by forcefitting it into the mold of the non-Christian system). A system is biblical only when it can be shown to have been built out of biblical materials in accordance with biblical principles, presuppositions, and practices.
6. Of course ordination in itself is no guarantee. Paul warned ordained men (elders) not only about wolves from the outside who would "enter in among you" (Acts 20:29) but also about those *"from among yourselves"* who will "arise speaking distorted things to drag away disciples to follow them" (Acts 20:30). Yet ordained men at least have had to pass the scrutiny and evaluation of their peers and are held accountable to them.

Chapter 3—What Is Spiritual Discernment?
1. William F. Buckley, *The Jeweler's Eye* (New York: G.P. Putnam's Sons, 1969), pp. 9, 10.
2. George B. Duncan, *Wanting The Impossible* (Grand Rapids: Wm. B. Eerdmans Publishing Co., 1957), p. 11.
3. Charles Colson, *The Struggle for Men's Hearts and Minds* (Wheaton: Victor Books, 1986), pp. 6, 37.
4. Tony Walter, *Need: The New Religion* (Downers Grove: InterVarsity Press, 1985), p. 39.
5. The book is one of the finest that InterVarsity has published since it issued John R. Stott's book *The Christian Counter Culture*, a title that clearly set forth the teachings of Jesus in the Sermon on the Mount in antithesis to the world's teachings. Unfortunately, that good title has been changed.

Chapter 4—The Basic Problem
1. *Hippocrates, Vol. III, The Loeb Classical Library* (Cambridge: Harvard University Press, 1959), p. 256.
2. I Clement 34:1.
3. See Polycarp's *Letter to the Ephesians* 9:1, where he speaks of "obeying the *word of righteousness*."

Chapter 5—Concern to Discern
1. In Philippians 1:10 the word translated "pure" is literally

"sun-tested." What is held up to the sunlight of the Word of righteousness is found pure and free from admixture only when it is God's truth. According to God's mathematics, when you add you often subtract. If you add error to truth, to the extent that impurities permeate the truth, to that extent you no longer have truth or the power thereof.

Chapter 7—A Program

1. In *What to Do on Thursday* I listed 91 topics and some of the important passages that deal with those topics as a starting point for knowing where to locate themes in the Bible.
2. These are fully developed in *What to Do on Thursday*, pages 61 and 62. Also, pages 53 to 98 have a lot of information on how to interpret the Bible.
3. It is important to use at least three commentaries to insure that there is no significant difference of opinion. When they differ, you must decide, based on the evidence presented, which view, if any, is correct.
4. There is much about the process of implementation in *What to Do on Thursday*.

OTHER GOOD
HARVEST HOUSE READING

BLOW AWAY THE BLACK CLOUDS
by *Florence Littauer*

Florence Littauer helps the reader to come to terms with the emotional handicap of depression, offers practical insight on how to determine the cause—physical, psychological, or spiritual—and maps out the guidelines for constructive action to overcome depression.

BOUNCING BACK
Finding Acceptance in the Face of Rejection
by *William Coleman*

Rejection is coming, just like bad weather! How we cope with its devastating effects will mean the difference between success and failure in our lives. Best-selling author William Coleman explores with sensitivity and insight such topics as: types of rejection, preparing your children to handle rejection, self-rejection, bouncing back when you feel you can't. Coleman's compassionate approach and godly counsel will help you turn the hurt of rejection into building blocks for a healthy self-image.

FREEDOM FROM GUILT
by *Bruce Narramore* and *Bill Counts*

Silent condemnation cripples and enslaves many sensitive Christians. But there is freedom from both depression and fear of failure. The authors combine their insights to illuminate the path of complete forgiveness and self-acceptance.

HOW TO WIN OVER FEAR
by *John Haggai*

Fear is a pervasive and destructive influence in modern society. Everyone seems to be afraid of something. Dr. John Haggai explores the different types of fears, the essential prerequisites and formula for winning over fear, and God's power that is available to conquer fear.

HOW TO WIN OVER PAIN
by *John Haggai*

With the same clear insight and powerful answers that made HOW TO WIN OVER WORRY a bestseller for more than 20 years, John Haggai addresses the problem of pain in our lives. Covering the gamut from physical suffering to the emotional anguish of rejection, loneliness, death, or separation, HOW TO WIN OVER PAIN asks the hard questions of life and presents God's strong and loving answers to our hurt and pain.

OVERCOMING HURTS AND ANGER
by *Dr. Dwight Carlson*

Dr. Carlson shows us how to confront our feelings and negative emotions in order to experience liberation and fulfillment. He presents seven practical steps to help us identify and cope with our feelings of hurt and anger.

PRIVATE PAIN
Healing for Hidden Hurts
by *Rich Wilkerson*

Rich Wilkerson, author of TEENAGERS: PARENTAL GUIDANCE SUGGESTED, tells us that "Few are exempt from some degree of private pain." Private pain may be emotional isolation, a sense of rejection, guilt, loneliness, depression, or other forms of inner anguish kept hidden from others. A book that offers help and understanding and shows how suffering and pain are the tools in the great Master Sculptor's plan for our lives.

THE PURPOSE OF SUFFERING
Knowing the God Who Comforts
by *Dr. H. Edwin Young*

A recent Gallup poll revealed that the most frequently asked question in America is, "Why do people suffer?" Dr. H. Edwin Young takes the reader through the book of Job for God's answer. He rejects the simplistic doctrines prevalent today that state, "You are suffering because of sin . . . God is punishing you!" and "As a child of God you can have complete health, wealth, and success just for the asking." Instead, he points the way to the sovereign God who alone can comfort us and show us THE PURPOSE OF SUFFERING.

Another *Provocative* Book by
Bestselling Author
JAY ADAMS

To receive our free catalog with information about this and
other Harvest House books, please fill in your name and
address below.

Name   _____

Address _____

         _____

Send to: **Harvest House Publishers**
               1075 Arrowsmith
               Eugene, Oregon 97402

DATE DUE

FEB 1 6 2017
FEB 1 7 2017